THE JOY OF TEACHING

There is a destiny that makes us brothers;
* None goes his way alone:*
All that we send into the lives of others
* Comes back into our own.*

—EDWIN MARKHAM

THE
JOY
OF
TEACHING

PEPRONIA MERJANIAN

United Church Press
Philadelphia • *Boston*

To the memory of my parents

Copyright © 1966
UNITED CHURCH PRESS

Library of Congress Catalog Card Number 66-23991

Preface

Teaching is intentional living. It calls into action the teacher's hidden potential, vitality, and courage, transcending his fears and anxieties, thus paving the way to self-affirmation, wholeness, and renewal. In this sense teaching is a joy—a joy that enables the teacher to smile through his difficulties, a sentiment that breaks through the surface and wells up with deep contentment, lifting him above the emotion of sheer gaiety, laughter, and pleasure. Joy comes into being through self-involvement in meaningful processes and authentic person-to-person relationships.

This book is to pay tribute to teachers who have touched the lives of many growing children by sharing with them their own battle and their continuing discovery of the paths from doubt to faith, from despair to hope, from gloom to joy. It is also to affirm faith in the latent power and the will of man to give his life to a purpose that he recognizes to be worthy of his time and talent.

Each teacher at his level of experience and at the age level of his teaching will find ideas, illustrations, experiences that are applicable. They are the outcome of questions and answers teachers have sought and found through their own groping and probing. All the stories are true.

I wish to extend my deep gratitude to many friends, teachers, and ministers who encouraged me to undertake this challenging venture. They allowed me to put to test some of my ideas and worked with me patiently and with understanding. I mention only a few by name: Dr. and Mrs. Philip Anderson, Dr. Oliver Powell, Dr. Benton S. Gaskell, Dr. Edward F. Manthei, Dr. Kenneth E. Seim, the congregation of the First Congregational Church (United Church of Christ), Western Springs, Illinois, and the Rev. Fred O. Doty.

Special thanks go to Mrs. Harry Scoble and Mrs. Kent Taylor who labored with me with love and enthusiasm. Without their encouragement and assistance this book could not have been written.

It is my hope that the reading and the discussion of these topics will stimulate thought and further research for imaginative and creative teaching. The reader is urged to teach in his own way, to add his own footnote or write his own commentary. Artist-teachers are desperately needed. You can become one if you will!

—PEPRONIA MERJANIAN

Contents

Chapter One

Teaching Is an Invitation to Love

*Go therefore and make disciples of all nations,
. . . teaching them to observe all that I have
commanded you; and lo, I am with you always.*
—MATTHEW 28:19-20

THE ESSENTIAL MEANING OF TEACHING

Annie Sullivan's life as the teacher of Helen Keller is an immortal and moving oration. William Gibson, in his play *The Miracle Worker,* describes how a tormented, vicious, beastly, but intelligent child was released from the prison of her body to enter the hall of fame because of the dedication and loving concern of her teacher. Annie wrestled with Helen just as Jacob wrestled with the "man." She was determined to receive the blessing—the blessing of Helen's response to love. Annie's struggle was richly rewarded. Her love kindled love in Helen's heart and sparked her mind. Together they lived probing the deeper meanings of life, seeking answers to man's predicament. Their discourse became an exciting experience, where both transcended physical limitations and expressed gratitude and indebtedness to God and man for the beauty that is in life and in the living.

Teaching is a personal invitation to know God's love. The church school teacher plans to impart knowledge and provide experiences that evoke a positive response in the children. He knows that knowledge and experiences are insufficient and ineffective if they are merely parroted from a book without becoming the expression of his personal faith. The children are attracted to the gospel as it is lived and proclaimed. In the teacher's love and witness they see the love of God. They can read this gospel at any age and can understand and derive meaning from it to the level of their maturity. "We were ready to share with you not only the gospel . . . but also our own selves, for you had become very dear to us. . . . For you are our glory and joy" (1 Thess. 2:8, 20).

Teaching, therefore, points to the quality of knowledge, not the quantity—not more knowledge, as exciting as it is, but broader, deeper, and relevant knowledge that speaks to the child's needs in this day and age.

Teaching is an expression of appreciation. Each teacher owes much to countless men and women who not only *informed* him but *formed* him—his attitudes, his character. They gave him his dreams, fired his dormant raw materials, gave him courage to walk without fear. How well Albert Einstein expressed this:

> What an extraordinary situation is that of us mortals! Each of us is here for a brief sojourn; for what purpose he knows not, though he sometimes thinks he feels it. But from the point of view of daily life, without going deeper, we exist for our fellowmen—in the first place for those on whose smiles and welfare all our happiness depends, and next for all those unknown to us personally with whose destinies we are bound up by the tie of sympathy. A hundred times every day I remind myself

that my inner and outer life depend on the labors of other men, living and dead, and that I must exert myself in order to give in the same measure as I have received and am still receiving. I am . . . often oppressed by the feeling that I am engrossing an unnecessary amount of the labor of my fellowmen.[1]

There is a yearning in each person to give his life to what is worthy. The teacher's commitment to penetrate into the life of his pupils expresses his response to his faith in the greatness of human nature. When the self is deeply involved in the act of genuine caring, there is hardly room for feelings of "quiet desperation"; rather, hardships, pain, and suffering can be used "as a means by which joy may be wrung out of existence."[2]

Every person is entrusted with a mission, the mission of caring for someone else. If he transmits to others a glimpse of the truth, the beauty, the goodness, and the love he has received with gratitude, life becomes abundantly filled with the true joy of living.

Teaching is guiding the learner to self-discovery. The vastness of problems and feelings of inadequacy and vagueness about inner resources lead man to self-distrust and disillusionment. The teacher, aware of the universality of this concern, exposes his pupil to the lives of men eminent in the past and the present— men of character and integrity who sought purpose for their lives and labored for its fulfillment. Such exposure and nurture can challenge the person to cultivate his own potential and urge him to realize in his own life the meaning of the saying "What man has done, man can do." "The ancestor of every action is thought," said Emerson. When the pupil's mind is stretched by knowledge

---

[1] Albert Einstein, *Ideas and Opinions* (New York: Crown Publishers, 1954), p. 8. Used by permission of the trustees of the Albert Einstein Estate.

[2] Joseph Wood Krutch, *The Modern Temper* (New York: Harcourt, Brace & Co., 1929), p. 87.

of great lives, it can never again be reduced to its original dimension.

Every child has talent, great or small, in some area, and he needs to be aware of it and use it. As Henry Thoreau said, God has not sent us into the world without some spending money. Talent and energy should be used where they count in the total scheme of life.

Teaching is helping the child to know God as his contemporary. God is not the voice from the dim past who made his ways known to priests and prophets. God is here and now, waiting to be known by all those who want to recognize the authority ever present to guide and give impetus to all man's strivings. Rabbi Abraham Heschel, professor of philosophy and religion at Jewish Theological Seminary in New York, pointed to the apathy of modern man in an address[3]: "People live as though they are dead. They need entertainment because there is no celebration in their hearts. Like Job, man says today, 'Lo, he passes by me, and I see him not.'" In a tone that expressed his bewilderment Rabbi Heschel added, "To be a contemporary of God and not to have met him!"

How exciting it is for us teachers to know God as our contemporary! Knowing God personally brings such vitality and power to our message that we want to tell our pupils what God has done for us.

THE MASTER TEACHER

"Seeing the crowds, he went up on the mountain. . . . And he opened his mouth and taught them" (Matt. 5:1-2). These words introduce the collection of Jesus' sayings that have come to be known as the Sermon on the Mount. But Jesus' ministry was not confined to formal teaching; every relationship, every event

---

[3] Delivered in Chicago, November 18, 1962, at a national convention on religious education.

was a learning-teaching situation. He was the Master Teacher, possessed with a high degree of sensitivity to men, women, and children. He dined with Zacchaeus, a rejected tax collector, and his acceptance of him as a son of God with great potential for good transformed him completely. He did not despise or condemn the woman who had sinned much because he saw in her the divine capacity to love and love deeply. In his busy schedule he had time for children, and in each one he saw a child of God. In every relationship he took a man by the hand and led him to God. When his followers wrote about him, they understood the full meaning of his words "He who has seen me has seen the Father."

Jesus spoke with eloquence and yet with simplicity and sincerity. He spoke with authority because he had an intimate knowledge of the economic, social, and political pressures—the vital everyday facts. He spoke with objectivity and with good judgment, using his rational mind in interpreting events. He spoke without fear, pointing to the consequences of evil and violence. He spoke with love and compassion, feeling in his heart men's sufferings and loneliness.

Man was the object and subject of his concern, man as an individual and mankind as a whole; and he reached man wherever he was—rich or poor, wise or foolish, saint or sinner. He spoke from collective, familiar experiences, using imagery, symbols, analogy. He spoke of the sheep and the shepherd, the sower and the seed, the wheat and the tares, the yeast and the dough, the vine and the vinedresser. Simple words, but pregnant with meaning! His message was sometimes obvious or explicit; on other occasions the meaning was hidden. The listeners had much to think about and debate. Jesus left room for imagination, room for thought. He wanted men to seek and to find. He knew that when meanings are personally discovered, they are meanings internalized and treasured. His hearers were under the spell of his enthusiasm. When he called men to follow him, they asked no questions. They knew they followed a teacher who knew the way and the truth.

Jesus was not preoccupied with trivial matters. He spoke about ultimate issues—the kingdom of God and the nature and principles that govern this kingdom. He invited his hearers to enter the kingdom. This concept could have sounded abstract but he *housed* the abstract ideas, gave them concrete bodies and forms using familiar analogies—the kingdom of heaven is like a householder who went out to hire laborers; the kingdom of heaven may be compared to a king who wished to settle accounts with his servants. His examples came from daily life—family, business, labor, authority, success, pressures. There was aliveness in his teachings, stirring a man from inside and making him want to dedicate himself to a worthy cause.

After two thousand years, Jesus still remains the Master Teacher. His message is as true today as it was in his day; his words kindle a flame of devotion.

In 1940 Albert Schweitzer wrote to a friend from Africa:

> When as a child I first heard of the kingdom of God, I was profoundly moved. And always I have carried the thought of the kingdom of God in my heart. I consider myself happy to be able to serve his kingdom with thoughts and activities. Some day these thoughts will take root anew in the hearts of men. It is this certitude which gives me the courage to live in this day so terrifying to pass through.[4]

SCIENTIFIC APPROACH TO TEACHING

Pupils are attracted not only to a teacher's wealth of knowledge but also to his love of knowledge, to his warmth and sincerity. They will not tolerate emotional distance between them.

---

[4] Quoted in Allan A. Hunter, "Albert Schweitzer at Eighty," *Advance,* January 12, 1955, p. 28.

This natural relationship enables the teacher to enter into the inner world of the pupil, well aware of the great storehouse of psychic energy within reach, waiting to be put to use. Through conversation he draws out ideas and feelings that have been imprisoned there. He listens patiently; he respects the thoughts and feelings that are expressed. The teacher is always conscious of the age characteristics of his pupils and their level of maturity. Since words are symbols, they can only partially signify what he hopes to say. Therefore, he chooses words wisely, at first using familiar ones and then gradually moving with the pupil to the unfamiliar and more complex words. Teachers who have read widely can make their teaching exciting and vital. Paracelsus, a sixteenth-century Swiss physician noted for his wide knowledge of chemistry and alchemy, said, "He who knows nothing loves nothing. He who can do nothing understands nothing. He who understands nothing is worthless. But he who understands also loves, notices, sees. . . . The more knowledge is inherent in a thing, the greater the love."[5]

In many respects a teacher is like a scientist. He has a holy curiosity and an inquiring mind. He searches for truth wherever he can find it—in the Scriptures, in manuals, in audiovisual aids, music, resource materials, and resource people. He learns to use his critical and objective judgment to differentiate evidence from interpretation, fact from fiction. He looks for cause-and-effect relationships as he observes life and experiences. And after reflection he selects and organizes his material in an orderly and intelligent manner.

There is no one sure way of teaching. Broad knowledge makes a teacher flexible and open-minded—the wider his knowledge, the greater his ability to be experimental. He does not say, "We have never done this before" or "That will never work." Instead he ventures into the unknown like a man of research to solve

---

[5] Paracelsus, *Selected Writings* (New York: Pantheon Books, 1951), p. 237.

one more problem. The resourceful teacher allows room for trial and error because he and the children can learn from their errors as much as from their successes, when the method used or the result obtained is honestly and critically appraised.

TEACHING, AN ART

A learned man is not necessarily a good teacher. He may possess all the needed knowledge, screen the information, "speak in the tongues of men and of angels," "understand all mysteries," yet sound like "a noisy gong or a clanging cymbal." Transmittal of knowledge does not guarantee learning.

A successful teacher is more than a scientist. He is an artist who goes beyond intelligence into the realm of insight and wisdom. He knows what is worth learning and what needs to be interpreted and translated into meaningful experience. The teacher through his personality and enthusiasm breathes his life into the subject matter to give it a new existence. Paint, canvas, and brush, when selected wisely and used intelligently, can change the uninteresting raw materials into a composition that expresses beauty and harmony in color and design. The sensitive teacher in his concern for the total picture wants to make sure that the bits of knowledge given in fragments are fitted into a whole. He sees through his eyes and feels within his heart the design and purpose for his teaching. There is an interaction between himself and the subject matter. He uses his imagination, his insights, his initiative, his personal touch; he uses his own brush to stimulate thought in his pupils. This type of teaching cannot be taught to others; it must be cultivated by each individual teacher. "What is the beauty in the landscape but a certain fertility in me," said Thoreau. He added, "We see as much as we possess."

The creative teacher encourages self-expression and rejoices in the variety of views he receives. A child dares to be different and still feels accepted. The teacher who encourages initiative and originality raises the attention level of the child. He is now actively involved in the learning process. He is a participant, not a spectator, learning what truly counts for him. Rapport develops between the teacher and learner, transfusing vitality and strength. The teacher's enthusiasm stimulates a response that enhances the child's desire to achieve his best. Then learning becomes a cause for celebration. A Russian educator sums this up: "A student is not a vessel to be filled, but a lamp to be lighted."[6]

THE DEMANDS OF TEACHING

A blacksmith taught the secrets of his trade to a young man who was forced to learn. The blacksmith commented, "I taught him all I knew but I failed to kindle a spark."

Artists tell us that the best art comes from the most difficult medium. It is easy to mold wax or clay and give it the desired pattern; working with marble requires skilled craftsmanship, patience, and understanding. But what a difference in the product!

Teachers enjoy working with pupils who are obedient, courteous, attentive, and helpful; they resent the one who argues and defies authority. Partly in jest they say, "I wish *he* were absent more often." The teacher is often tempted to use some quick device to cut the "clown" down to size. Threats may temporarily bring the child to his senses, but he becomes a disturbance again the following Sunday. He cannot be motivated because his immediate need for love and acceptance exceeds his desire for learning.

Children have to be heard and accepted if teaching is to bear fruit. We can learn from the wisdom of the past: "There is no

---

[6] Editorial, *Life* magazine, September 28, 1962, p. 4.

fear in love, but perfect love casts out fear" (1 John 4:18). "Love is patient and kind . . . ; it is not irritable or resentful. Love bears all things, . . . endures all things" (1 Cor. 13:4-5, 7).

Teaching is never easy. It is a labor of love. No one can learn how to teach in five or ten easy lessons. Teaching demands self-sacrifice and priority in the hierarchy of values. It challenges the whole being.

In a charge to graduates, Russell Henry Stafford, president emeritus of Hartford Seminary Foundation, said, "We love because he first loved us. Whom we love we will serve, and whom we love, and they alone, we can serve to their good and our own."

To love the unlovely is a taxing job. When the teacher is aware of the seriousness of his obligation he uses all his skills to reach the child, but at times he feels he has not even come close to touching him. He goes home feeling completely empty and defeated, and his anxiety and despair continue through the week. He must ask the questions: What should I have done to reach him? How and where did I fail? What assuring words could I have used? How can I arouse his interest? A reasonable amount of dissatisfaction is necessary for growth if one is to learn from failure. Toynbee calls this "withdrawal and return"—the need for a person to look and then to think.

The teacher who does not often experience agony has never known ecstasy. He is perhaps the happy-go-lucky teacher. But there will always be a gap between what we teachers think teaching ought to be and what actually happens in the classroom. This realization helps us to reach upward toward the idea we gradually hope to achieve. Some teachers are emotionally paralyzed when faced with real challenges; they give up their mission with a feeling of defeat; they often have false expectations of themselves and of their children. Transformation does not happen in one or two days; it is a continuing process, perhaps almost unnoticed, like the growth of a plant.

The teacher's task is to sow the seed, unhurriedly, lovingly, and to wait for the sun and the rain to unfold what is stored in that seed. God needs the cooperation and stamina of teachers to work out his purposes with his children. "I planted, Apollos watered, but God gave the growth. So neither he who plants nor he who waters is anything, but only God who gives the growth. . . . For we are fellow workmen with God" (1 Cor. 3:6-7, 9).

The teacher who feels the challenge in teaching also feels the joy, as shown by this excerpt from a letter written by a teacher from her hospital bed: "I have had the thrill and enrichment of teaching this fall and winter. It has been a struggle—no question about that—but what isn't that is really rewarding in life."

"Teaching is the most thankless job," is often heard. Teachers in church schools do not make headline news. There is no glamour attached to their work; no one plays the trumpet or blows the bugle for them. But the teacher who is devoted to his mission is above this need for glory. He experiences the deep, intense joy of becoming an instrument in the hand of God, used to guide a pupil to discover himself as a child of God. Teaching in this sense is truly an investment of the whole self—but what a dividend!

Teaching is a journey, and each traveler has to find the road to his goal. One or two sessions do not determine the quality of teaching. Robert Browning's words can be a great help:

> Success is a journey, not a destination.
> Just as courage is the conquest of fear,
> So greatness is measured as
> Triumph over circumstances.

REMEMBERED TEACHERS

Miss Senem, our mathematics teacher, asked if we students would be willing to come during our Christmas vacation to hear the story *The Other Wise Man* by Henry Van Dyke. The classrooms were locked, the janitor not available. It was a stormy afternoon. We sat under a leaking tin roof on hard benches in the corridor and watched the radiant face of the delicate woman as she started to unfold the plot of the story. She talked as though she believed in every word, and she made us believe too. I was in the fifth grade then in Beirut, Lebanon. After these many years, this little woman still stands tall in my memory.

As we who teach turn back through the pages of our life's album, we recall with reverence and love men and women who have inspired us to become what we are. We owe to all of them a debt of gratitude. The world looks better to those of us who have been touched by such lives.

Ezra Poulsen remembers with gratitude Prof. Alfred Osmond, who said to a student, "Young man, I want you to understand, you're not a finished product. You're still in the process of being created."[7] These words gave courage to the hesitant author, and he continued to write successful poetry, fiction, and biography.

New York Judge Irving Ben Cooper paid tribute to a high school teacher:

> I could almost feel [her] presence there in my chambers, and see her nod of approval because I had just given a boy what she had once given me.
>
> I had never known kindness, but she taught me that most people are kind and decent.
>
> "Poverty of mind and spirit is as awful as poverty of the body. . . . Serve *with* honor and not *for* honor. . . . Bring your religion into the thick of the world and put it to work there."[8]

A high school student expressed his love for his teacher in this way: "He enjoyed teaching us boys. He never acted as if this was just another job. We felt that he was not only a teacher but also our friend."

---

[7] Ezra J. Poulsen, "Words to Live By," *This Week* magazine, September 16, 1962, p. 2.

[8] Irving Ben Cooper, "Salute to a Teacher," *Reader's Digest,* June, 1957, pp. 155, 160.

The pupil uses simple, clear language to express his need for love, understanding, recognition, respect, security, courage. The teacher can satisfy these needs in diverse ways. He can follow up on the assignments, call on the sick child, send a card to the absent. In the classroom he can make a child feel that his ideas and efforts count. He can praise work that is done well, so that the child may grow in self-trust and self-respect.

Peter and Andrew heard the call of Jesus: "Follow me, and I will make you fishers of men." Feeling his love, they responded to him. They followed him to street corners and synagogues, into the upper room and before the authorities of the state. They told everyone what they heard and saw, feeling their teacher's approval and declaring their dependence on God for insight, wisdom, and direction.

WITNESSING IN THE WILDERNESS

Stephen, speaking to the high priest and the council, said, "Our fathers had the tent of witness in the wilderness" (Acts 7:44). Teachers are confronted today with the awesome responsibility of preparing children for a life of uncertainty. Cold and hot wars, space-age competition bring us back to the wilderness. But in this wilderness there is an oasis, "the tent of witness." As teachers we must be intensely alive to the significance of the moment. To be aware of the present as God's time and to be sensitive to the needs of God's children now, means to fill time with meaning and to find fulfillment in life. The sharing of one's self to the fullest with another enhances and enriches both the giver and the receiver, and together they experience the joy of bringing into existence new life infinitely greater than that which either could have hoped for separately.

Chapter Two

Know the Child

*I am the good shepherd; I know my own [sheep]
and my own know me. . . . My own sheep hear
my voice, and I know them, and they follow me.*

—JOHN 10:14, 27

WHAT IS YOUR NAME?

Eugene Ionesco's one-act play *The Leader* makes a person think
deeply. The principal character, called the Leader, in all his
pomp and glory, is parading in the distance with his entourage.
He is shaking hands, being photographed, signing autographs.
People admire every gesture he makes. The contagion of excitement spreads. Frenzied hurrahs run through the crowd, rising in
crescendo. Then one by one the admirers are stunned to see that
the Leader is headless. One spectator cries, "What's he need a
head for if he's a genius!" The playwright makes his sad commentary on our irrational culture when each of his characters
shouts loudly and indifferently to another and then all in chorus,
"What is your name?" "What is your name?" "What is your

name?" No one waits for an answer; no answer is given; no one *cares* to know the answer. Each one is just asking a question.

WHAT'S IN A NAME?

Mr. and Mrs. Andrew Adams bring their baby to the altar to be baptized.

The minister asks, "By what name shall this child be called?"

The father replies with pride and affection, "Andrew Adams, the Second."

The minister holds the baby gently, looks at the smiling face, and prays in his heart when he says, "Andrew Adams, I baptize you in the name of the Father, and of the Son, and of the Holy Spirit. Amen."

Andrew Adams now has identity. He belongs to the household of God, a believing and witnessing community. He is received into the loving fellowship of his church to be nurtured in the ways of the Lord. His name gives him a knowledge of his heritage, a purpose, and a mission.

THE CHILD'S SEARCH FOR IDENTITY

The growing child finds himself in a confusing culture where people live in indifference. The picture of society described by adults disturbs him. He hears condemnation in their voices as they call each other name-droppers, status-seekers, mask-wearers.

He is surrounded by contemporary art, which portrays a decadent society where men and women have no form or shape. If he can recognize the form of a person in all this splash and dripping color, the anatomy is often dislocated, the head skull-like, and the body shadowy or skeletal. The artist is true to his vision. His vivid and prophetic denunciations of man's inhumanity to man alarm sensitive viewers. They share the artist's agony and gloom. Other spectators, equally sincere, find hostility and violence in these expressions. They reject this "new realism" as false, distorted, and unintelligible. They realize that this age has its own brand of anxiety, that there are men and women who live meaningless lives and are pressured by meaningless chores—but that there are also dedicated people, overflowing with compassion, who work day and night and try to improve today for a better tomorrow.

As a child matures, he looks, reads, and listens intently in order to understand the deeper meanings of these contradictory insights, and he wonders about himself and his place in society:

> Twinkle, twinkle, little star
> How I wonder what I are.

WAYS TO KNOW THE CHILD

"These are your children," says the church school superintendent as she warmly greets the hesitant teacher. The teacher picks up his packet and reads the names: Craig Stephens, Claudia Curtis, Heidi Heyden—names, so impersonal and distant. As he works with these children, he becomes increasingly aware of his glorious responsibility to put himself wholly into his task. He is fully aware that he will get out of his experience what he puts into it—knowledge, purpose, meaning. He recognizes that, although each child shares in that irreducible quality which exists in each person after differences have been stripped away, he is unique. The teacher wrestles with such questions as: Who is he? What are his needs? How do I meet these needs?

Recently while substituting in the third grade, I called the names of the children from their cards. If I knew the child I read his name and looked at him. When a name was unfamiliar, I waited for the child to answer. I called the name of a bright but restless boy, and looked at him and smiled. He bent over to his friend and whispered, "She knows my name; she loves me."

Name tags, playing games, sharing of interests and hobbies give the pupil a sense of identity and self-affirmation. He is known by his name and loves to be called by his name.

Records. The Pupil's Interest Record on page 26 is for use in a personal interview. It can be revised to suit particular needs and interests. It introduces the child so that the teacher can communicate with him intelligently. Many bored children have regained vitality and interest when the teacher said, "Pat, I know you've done a lot of reading about Abraham Lincoln; tell us about his emancipation program" or "Johnny, you're president of your space club. When is the next launching of a space capsule?" This kind of relationship breaks down barriers; the child knows his teacher is interested in him.

The evaluation form on pages 27-28 can also be adapted. It was prepared by the chairman of the board of Christian education of a local church, who is a professor of psychology. He had met with teachers, listened to their needs, and looked carefully at the curriculum. Some teachers have used the form successfully twice during the year—at the beginning and again at the end—to discover evidence of change or growth. Such information will never reveal the whole story of a particular child, but it may open windows and cast some light. If this information needs to be shared, teachers must use their best judgment in its interpretation.

Role-playing. Role-playing can be used effectively with juniors and adolescents. It gives the teacher an insight into patterns of behavior of a particular age-group and the peer-group mores of acceptance and rejection. The children also understand more clearly the feelings of each member of the group. And when an individual expresses his idea aloud, he hears himself clearly, crystallizes his thinking, and can then make more intelligent judgments. (See pages 71-72 for a fuller discussion of role-playing.)

Creative writing. Adolescent students can be asked to write two paragraphs about their understanding of a problem. For example, Lucy was invited by her boyfriend to go to the movies at eight o'clock in the evening. Her mother did not permit her to go. How did Lucy feel, and what happened?

Pupil's Interest Record[1]
(Recorded by the teacher in a personal interview)

Name_____ Date_____ Grade_____

1. Names of brothers and sisters:

2. With whom would you like to work?
   (1)_____ (2)_____ (3)_____
   With whom would you like to play?
   (1)_____ (2)_____ (3)_____

3. If you were going to be in a show or play, what kind of person would you like to pretend to be? Why?

4. If you were going to pretend to be an animal, what animal would you like to be? Why?

5. What would you like to be when you grow up? Why?

6. What subject do you like best in school? What subject do you like least?

7. If you could have three wishes that could come true, what would you wish?
   (1)
   (2)
   (3)

8. Most children sometimes feel afraid. What are some of the things that make you feel afraid?

9. What would you like different at home? At school?

---

1 Prepared by Donald Dinkmeyer, professor of psychology, National College of Education, Evanston, Illinois. Used by permission.

Observation Record[2]

Name_____ Grade_____

Teacher_____ Date_____

This report will serve as a record of the child's development during the year. The checklist is to point up what relatively strong points the child possesses. An unchecked item would not necessarily mean a weakness in that area. A double check stands for outstanding ability.

1. Personal attributes (attitudes, talents)
   ___Friendly
   ___Thoughtful of others
   ___Contributes to group thinking
   ___Shows originality in group thinking
   ___Shows leadership qualities: initiative, creativity, self-confidence
   ___Enjoys carrying out assignments
   ___Enjoys bringing materials for group projects
   ___Enjoys spending time outside of church school on projects

   Has special talent in:

   Oral expression: dramatization___ reading aloud___ story-telling___
   Written expression: prose___ poetry___
   Arts and crafts: drawing___ painting___ woodwork___ paper construction___
   Music: instrumental___ vocal___ appreciation___
   Other outstanding attributes_____

2. Does he seem to enjoy the program as a whole? Yes___ No___

---

[2] Prepared by Edward Minium, professor of psychology, State College, San Jose, California. Used by permission.

3. Does he seem to enjoy any particular part of the program?
   Lesson discussion___ Music___ Worship___ Educational
   activities___ Social contacts___

4. If he does not enjoy the program, have you any ideas why?

5. How frequently does he attend?
   Regularly (barring illness and family activity)___ Spas-
   modically___ Seldom___

6. Further comments:

This type of writing helps the teacher to understand relationships at home, the degree of acceptance and rejection of authority, values and mores the family holds and cherishes, and the
amount of freedom and repression the individual child feels.

A student may be asked to write five things he likes best and
five he dislikes. This aids in understanding a child's values. A
student may be asked to write paragraphs on "I would like to be
like Mr._____ or Mrs._____ because_____" or "I am like Mr.
_____ or Mrs._____ because_____." Writing in response to pictures
is also a helpful technique.

Creative drawing. Drawings reveal a child's response to his
environment—parents, brothers and sisters, school, playmates. His
choice of colors and content will throw some light on how he reacts to these areas in his life. A happy child usually uses bright
colors, but there *are* some happy children who enjoy working
with black crayons. Color alone does not determine a child's
inner anxiety or serenity, joy or fear. What he tells about his
picture and with what feeling tone he expresses himself, what he
intentionally or hesitatingly includes or omits in his description
will give a clearer understanding of his goals and values.

Visiting the home. Enrico was a small boy when I met him

eleven years ago. He flashed his big black piercing eyes, gave me one quick smile, and ran as fast as he could from one end of the nursery room to the other. He was alive and alert, and I watched him with interest. But sometimes Enrico annoyed me. He grabbed the toys of other children; and if he met resistance, he fought with his fists or threw himself on the floor in temper tantrums.

One day I was his victim when I tried to prevent his hitting a smaller boy. With hatred in his eyes, he bit my arm. When I saw the red round impression left by his teeth, my first impulse was to retaliate. But I would never hurt a child sick with pneumonia or heart disease; Enrico was emotionally sick. How would I cope with this situation? I called Enrico's mother and made an appointment.

Enrico's mother was pleased to see me. She told me about her son's brain concussion suffered in a car accident. This shocking experience had made him restless, aggressive, and somewhat mean. Through tension-release toys—pegs that could be hammered into holes, clay to be molded, finger painting, soap bubbles in a small tub of water—Enrico was gradually able to express his hostilities and get rid of his negative impulses.

A call in the home of each pupil will evoke a warm and appreciative response. What the child experiences in genuine relationships will be remembered in the future with quiet affection.

Listening. A demonstration school had provided an unusually gratifying week. The fellowship had grown intimate as the staff had worked and shared together. The children had become more open and responsive.

Larry was the "boy with problems," the object of concern. The members of the staff watched him quietly, extending every courtesy and kindness they could without making him conscious of their awareness of his needs. He was assigned, with three other boys, to draw the map of Asia Minor, trace Paul's three journeys, locate important cities, and discover through research the important events that had taken place in each one. He took the poster right away, traced the map accurately, and signed his name in the left-hand corner of the map. One of the boys working with him disliked this gesture. He whispered to the others, "He is always like that." The teacher asked the other boys to sign their names too.

On Friday afternoon, the last hour of the last day, an open house for parents was being planned. The teacher who worked closely with Larry was sitting near the map. Larry came to her, and I overheard this conversation:

Larry: I don't know who I am. I don't know who my mother is.

Teacher: Don't you have a mother, Larry?

Larry: Yes, I do, but she is not my real mother. Mother died when I was two years old.

Teacher: I'm sure she was a wonderful person to be your mother.

Larry: No, she wasn't. My father divorced her.

Teacher: I'm sure the mother you have now is a fine person.

Larry: She is all right, I guess.

Teacher: You are a fine boy, Larry.

Larry: But I don't know who I am. *(Turning to me)* Are we going to have a lab school next year? I will be here again.

Educators are alert to discover what the child really thinks he is like. What is his self-image? How does he see himself in relation to his peer group? He carries his self-concept into all his relationships. From his vantage point he acts and reacts positively or negatively to a situation.

The teacher listens to the pupil with interest when he comes to tell his story. The child wants to share his anxieties because the teacher has inspired his confidence. The child may show exaggeration, doubt, or overt sureness in his words; his *feeling tone* may reveal his fears, hurts, and frustrations. The distorted image he gives of himself may be the reflection of adults' attitudes toward him. This is the teacher's chance to release him from the emotional exhaustion that has led him to despair. This is the teacher's opportunity to love him and heal him. The child's story is his confidence and is sacred to him. A sensitive teacher will not abuse it or treat it as a trivial matter.

Social experiences. Field trips in relation to the course of study; social functions, such as parties, picnics, hikes, breakfasts, theater parties, football and baseball games—all are extracurricular activities that demand the second mile from teachers. Through these relationships the child grows to know his teacher as a person and finds himself an interested participant. The seed that the teacher sows now falls on more fertile soil.

Age characteristics. In this poem the elfman is saying that his development and growth should not be compared to someone else's.

> I met a little elfman, once
> Down where the lilies blow.
> I asked him why he was so small
> And why he did not grow.
>
> He slightly frowned and with his eyes
> He looked me through and through.
> "I'm quite as big for me," he said,
> "As you are big for you."
> —John Kendrick Bangs[3]

As the teacher observes children, he needs to have the approach of the developmental psychologist who recognizes that:

1. Each child has his own rate of growth. Judy at four can ride her tricycle; Johnny cannot. But when he is ready physically and with the proper motivation and interest, he will ride.

2. The rate of growth is uneven and gradual. There are

---

[3] John Kendrick Bangs, "The Elfman." Used by permission of Hanneli H. Moché.

periods of rapid and slow growth. With each stage in his development, as his interests change, the child is capable of performing tasks he was unable to perform previously.

These techniques, these ways of studying children, do not provide the teacher with a "bag of tricks" to serve as a cure-all; they will, however, increase his understanding of the child and help him develop more constructive feelings. But knowledge itself is not enough. *It is what you do with what you know that truly counts.*

Michelangelo, strolling in the outskirts of Rome, found a piece of dirty marble. When he picked it up and looked at it with admiration, his friends asked why he was interested in such trash. The artist replied, "In that dirty stone I see the face of an angel."

The child is not a piece of marble that can be chiseled after a pattern. He will rebel, resist, and fight all forms of manipulation. The wise teacher believes in his infinite worth as a child of God. He will accept him as he is—even though temporarily marred—and guide him to a discovery of his potential, his origin and destiny.

In relationships where he encounters genuine love, the child comes home to himself and finds his true nature, the image his Maker gave him at birth. When we teachers witness this miracle, our hearts are filled with gratitude for being called to this ministry.

WHAT ARE THE CHILD'S NEEDS?

The child who needs individualized help does not necessarily have a low IQ or have to be exposed to the tyranny of poverty which paralyzes him emotionally. What are the other forces that act upon him to make him unable to reach out? How does a child form his self-concept?

The role of nature. The child inherits his raw materials from his family. He is equipped with a certain degree of ability. Some things he does skillfully, others satisfactorily or even poorly. He also inherits his physical appearance—handsome or ugly, healthy or handicapped. A child may carry wounds deep in his heart.

The role of nurture. Parents influence the way in which a child acquires his self-concept. He is not born with an image of himself as good or bad, capable or weak. Even before he can think or reason or have any concept of the "I," he can feel love and warmth. Occasional harsh words, a few angry looks or misunderstandings, well-deserved punishment will not leave eternal scars. But *consistency* in approval or disapproval, in acceptance or rejection, immeasurably influences his image of himself. *A child is the sum total of his experiences.* The following stories illustrate the effect parents' attitudes have on children.

Twelve-year-old Harry was in the fifth grade. He looked pale and weak and showed no interest in schoolwork. He loved drawing, but his ability in art was never recognized or capitalized on by his teachers. He failed all his courses. He felt out of place and gloomy. A cruel remark by his peers brought hysterical tears.

Harry's mother was alternately offensive and defensive at school, a headache to the staff. She attacked the school and accused the teachers of lack of ingenuity in their failure to understand her bright child's abilities. She refused to accept his failures; she felt they were her own.

"You should be ashamed of yourself!" cried Fred's mother. "You are twice as big as Carl. He made a home run and you didn't even hit the ball." Fred's heart sank, and he did not even look at her.

At home the mother continued, "What's wrong with you anyway? Why can't you be like Carl?"

Fred went to his room and threw himself on his bed. The words echoed harshly, cruelly, "Why can't you be like Carl? Why can't you be like Carl?"

Elize was a talented, attractive student; she had a lovely singing voice and was an accomplished pianist for her age.

As a result of polio, Elize limped a little and had to wear corrective shoes. This was not a problem to her among her peers. But at home she talked very little and shared even less. She was sad. Each time she looked at her mother, she saw anxiety and pity. She knew her parents loved her deeply. They gave her every imaginable material thing. But the parents could not accept their child's handicap. This was an emotional burden she had to bear alone.

Jim was a handsome boy blessed with talented and loving parents, and his needs were met with understanding. He grew, knowing that he was loved, and from this knowledge he derived his sense of security. He developed faith in himself and others. Though he did well in school, he was denied membership in a club he wished to join; but this did not discourage him. He formed a club of his own and appointed himself president!

Parents have dreams and aspirations for their children, and rightly so. But if there is a discrepancy between a child's ability to perform and the standard of expectation of his parents, it often leads to a feeling of defeat. The parents' anxiety is real; but what a blessing when a secure home can help a child take frustration in stride!

School will also influence the child. He brings to it attitudes and values already in operation. He looks at his teacher and he is intent and baffled. He wonders how he will be rated as a person and how he should respond to authority. His ideas are challenged, his actions screened, his words censored. New and wider experiences open up. Will he have the courage to plunge into the unknown? Or will he withdraw from lack of confidence?

He may succeed, or he may fail. One success may lead to another, each one reinforcing his sense of accomplishment and his self-concept. Or he may fail, yet have the courage to try again. But the child with a low measure of self-esteem will not venture on; any failure will reinforce his negative, impoverished self-concept.

The child is influenced by peer groups at all ages to a greater or less degree, but these pressures are dramatic during pre-adolescence. He is seeking a new status. So it is more important to him to obey the rules and regulations set by his peers than those established by his parents; he moves toward dependence on group authority. He feels he has to know the codes and signals, wear the accepted type of clothing, ride his bike to school or walk, play the same records—all according to the dictated custom.

But while he needs to belong to a group for his identity, deep down he also wants to be a unique person, an individual loved for his own sake. However, he does not yet know how. He does not always approve the club codes; he wishes he had the nerve to stand out and disagree—but he cannot. So an inner battle rages. Outwardly he conforms; inwardly he rebels against his own weakness. This battle will continue through many years as his inner self and his outer self are becoming more integrated, and he is growing more sure of himself as a person in his own right.

David was standing outside the door of his classroom. The teacher had asked him to leave. There he was, groomed immaculately. I walked to him quietly and asked why he was not in the classroom. He must have been feeling sorry for himself; his eyes were full of tears. He said in a passionate voice, "I don't know why I do what I do. I *want* to do right, but I do the wrong thing."

I remembered the words of Paul when he spoke of his own battle: "I do not do the good I want, but the evil I do not want is what I do" (Rom. 7:19).

HOW ARE THE CHILD'S NEEDS MET?

The minister held a large sheet of paper before the children and asked, "What do you see?" Five children said, "An ink spot." "What else?" he asked. There was no answer. "You all missed seeing the large clean white paper!"

We label a child a *problem*. Actually, he is like the white sheet of paper with an ink spot. He *has* a problem. We need to think of him as a total being with positive and negative behavior. We need to bring to our aid all our knowledge of human personality, for the causes of his conflict may be varied—physiological, cultural, educational. In every case the problem points to a value that is important to the child and is unmet. These needs should be satisfied now so the child can look forward to a happy adulthood.

A child is educable; experience verifies this. Man can change radically. He can move toward the good at every stage of his life. This belief is based on years of work by competent people with disturbed children and adults. The belief should inspire hope in the teacher, and he can venture with faith to look at his task as a challenge and an opportunity entrusted to him by God, worthy or unworthy though he may feel. How well Paul says it to the Romans!

> We rejoice in our sufferings, knowing that suffering produces endurance, and endurance produces character, and character produces hope, and hope does not disappoint us, because God's love has been poured into our hearts through the Holy Spirit which has been given to us.   —Romans 5:3-5

This gift of love is an act of grace. It is not given because people deserve it, but rather to enable them to reach out in response to the continuing command: "Love one another as I have loved you."

Just what does the word love mean? At a seminar discussion the word love was put on the chalkboard. All participants agreed that the word is a concept and is formed by many ingredients which need to be defined. The following ideas were brought forth. Love is:

- Acceptance of other people no matter who they are.
- Concern for the needs of people, not only intellectual but emotional understanding.
- Care—actual extension of the self in acts of mercy and service.
- Respect, because each person is a child of God born with inalienable rights.
- Responsibility—a response to the needs of one's fellowmen in the manner in which we can best serve.
- Fellowship, where men are bound together with a common interest and faith and thus enter into a relationship with faith.
- Outreach—an urgency to reach out to others because this is one's mission.

None of these ideas expresses the whole truth in itself, but viewed together they show that to have love is to be in a dynamic state. This vitality gushes through a person like mighty waters. When children are exposed to love, they in turn feel revitalized and can channel their energies into meaningful experiences.

Love and encounter. The following points are helpful to the teacher as he puts love into action in the church school:

1. Diminish the psychological distance between yourself and the child. Talk to him as person to person with respect and understanding, without abdicating authority; share some of your past and present joys, fears, and the experiences of effort and discipline.

2. Give him honest and sincere recognition of work well done, verbally or with facial expression, in public or private, as you see fit.

3. Fair play is essential. The demanding child needs recognition. However, recognition is a universal need. Be alert to the needs of *all* children.

4. Talk to *each* child every Sunday. This will make him feel that you care about him, that he is important.

5. Bring to the classroom all the knowledge that you can acquire about the child, his limitations and capabilities, his interests and dislikes. Then you will have realistic expectations of each according to his ability. Where there is real concern, there is intelligent planning for all the children.

6. Your tone of voice, dead or alive, enthusiastic or despairing, sets the climate and mood for the quality of response you will receive. Set the stage for clear reception. Thomas Aquinas wisely said, "Everything that is received is received in the mood of the receiver."

7. Encourage satisfying interpersonal relationships. As simple an action as taking off your hat shows you are there to stay. Arrange your room to give children a feeling of belonging. Take away empty chairs. Plan together; share equipment and experiences. Watch especially for the shy child, who has a greater problem than an aggressive one. He withdraws into his shell and gradually fades away into nonidentity in the group.

The appearance of the classroom. An attractive room is always inviting. Children like to do their share in the arrangement of the furniture and the worship center; they have put something of themselves into the place and feel they belong. They may remove broken furniture, pick up the clutter on the piano, remove the oversized offering plate.

The relevance of the subject matter. The child wonders why he should spend so much time in studying men like Joseph, Moses, and Amos. He feels like saying, "Let the dead bury their dead." He would prefer to study about space-age scientists; this would be more exciting and relevant. The child's goals are immediate. He wants to know what is right and wrong conduct *now*. He is interested not in particular mores, but in moral and spiritual principles, so he can function with the least amount of fear and uncertainty.

Classroom discussions should lead the child to an understanding that these are universal problems wrestled with in every age; these were heroes faced with anxieties, conflicts, and decision-making problems similar to life-and-death questions today. They acted with courage and resolve; they responded to the call of God. Thus the teacher hopes that what at first appears as a meaningless historical event will become a present reality and the child will "go and do likewise."

THE GOOD NEWS

The preceding pages discuss the forces that influence a pupil's growth, the factors in his nature and nurture. But the *real self* is not created by these forces. There is another power within him— God, who enables him to react against conditions and conditioning. This power encourages him to live with his doubts when he labors with questions: What is truth? What is God's purpose for my life? What is my destiny? How does God redeem, forgive, and judge? He would prefer to find out for himself. The dialogue between God and himself sharpens his awareness of the divine spark within him.

This was Paul's experience, and he shared this assurance with his fellow doubters and believers: "It is the Spirit himself bearing witness with our spirit that we are children of God, and if children, then heirs, heirs of God and fellow heirs with Christ" (Rom. 8:16-17). Sonship takes away price tags. It gives a man a sense of personal worth.

To the plea of Larry, "I do not know who I am," the Bible proclaims the good news: Larry, fear not. You are a son of God; you are mine, and I know you by name.

William Blake, in his poem "The Lamb," voices both the quest and the answer to a child's search for identity:

> Little lamb, who made thee?
> Dost thou know who made thee,
> Gave thee life, and bade thee feed
> By the stream and o'er the mead;
> Gave thee clothing of delight,
> Softest clothing, wooly, bright;
> Gave thee such a tender voice,
> Making all the vales rejoice?
>   Little lamb, who made thee?
>   Dost thou know who made thee?
>
> Little lamb, I'll tell thee;
> Little lamb, I'll tell thee:
> He is callèd by thy name,
> For he calls himself a Lamb.
> He is meek, and he is mild,
> He became a little child.
> I a child, and thou a lamb,
> We are callèd by his name.
>   Little lamb, God bless thee!
>   Little lamb, God bless thee![4]

---

[4] *The Poetical Works of William Blake,* ed. William Michael Rossetti (London: G. Bell & Sons, Ltd., 1917), pp. 80 f.

Chapter Three

Learning

*Not I, not anyone else can travel that road
    for you,
You must travel it for yourself.*

—WALT WHITMAN[1]

WHAT IS LEARNING?

Learning is not the grasp or mastery of isolated facts. It is the perception of the interdependence of facts and life. It is a thought process which enables the learner to discover meaning through flashes of insight and by reflecting, interpreting, and translating knowledge into daily living.

Each generation finds it necessary to redefine learning. Despite extensive research in the field to determine how children and adults learn, very few conclusive results have been attained. Man is still a mysterious and complicated creature.

At every stage in his development, man is reaching out for contact with reality. Everything that he experiences as real is significant to him. Meaningful learning is the offspring of meaningful experiences. The joy he derives from such experiences

---

[1] Walt Whitman, "Song of Myself," *Leaves of Grass.*

evokes in him a passion for wider and more comprehensive out-reach toward reality. His love for the song of a bird will provide the incentive to find the name of the bird, its natural habitat, its reaction to heat and cold, its habit of migration. His knowledge of and interest in one bird will lead to the discovery of many birds.

The spontaneous curiosity of the learner about the real is grounded in an instinct for the rational, orderly, and beautiful. It is his impulse for life. The church school teacher will encourage and nurture this natural flow of enthusiasm in the areas where the student has a real love and desire to know; he will immerse himself in the life situation of his pupil, and together they will explore the many facets of his interest, looking for new avenues leading to the pupil's goal. The creative teacher will guide the seeker beyond the knowledge of facts. He will encourage him to make his abstractions, his generalizations, his interpretations as to what all this searching and finding really means to him. In a classroom where creative learning is fostered, the pupil will not be reluctant to express his thoughts and feelings. He will rely heavily on his own insights, right or wrong, fully aware that the teacher will understand and appreciate an honest search for truth.

Learning in this sense is a conversion experience, an actual change in the pupil's mind, feelings, actions, motives, and goals. An important change takes a long time to ripen into fruition. Each meaningful experience provides the fertile soil for a healthy craving for further contact with reality. Learning thus affirms man's belief in his own capacity and provides opportunities for self-fulfillment and self-discovery.

HOW CHILDREN LEARN

Children learn by involvement. A teacher often falsely assumes that when he tells a child what is right and wrong in his own eloquent manner, the pupil is bound to be impressed and want to change his behavior. Human nature rebels against being told. The child has both the need and the urge to make decisions in his own way and in his own time. He wants to engage in activities that will bring about new understanding, new insight, and new skills.

Pat, a seventh-grade pupil, shared her concern about her friend Ruth. "I am the only friend she has. I am the only one who has lunch with her. All the other kids stay away from her. She is not invited to any of the parties. They don't like her because she is smart . . . and Jewish. . . . Well, she can't help it. After school she goes home and studies the dictionary."

The seventh-graders decided to invite Ruth to their class on Brotherhood Sunday. Ruth gave an unusually well-prepared presentation of the meaning of brotherhood and the importance of understanding our indebtedness and interdependence to each culture for its unique contribution. In the question-and-answer period the youngsters discovered that Ruth was planning to be a journalist and was preparing herself for the attainment of her goal. For two months after this meaningful experience the class learned about the contributions of many cultures in the United States and neighboring countries. They climaxed the program by wearing the costumes of the people they had studied and displayed one product for which each country was famous. The script they wrote showed their genuine sensitivity and appreciation for all cultures.

These experiences provided many opportunities for personal involvement in making decisions about what country to study, in looking for material, in interviewing students from other lands, and in planning the display. The students began to understand what prejudice is, how it is born in the minds of people, and what they could do to uproot it.

In the preschool department the teachers are very earnest in engaging the child in activities in which he actually participates. The child is encouraged to touch, to smell, to feel, to play. He constantly asks questions about people and objects in his own environment. He is happy, alive, alert because he clearly identifies himself with his experiences.

As the child grows older, he develops the ability to see and to feel the impact of facts and ideas through the eyes of his mind. He has moved from the knowing-how-to-do stage to a more reflective period. He expresses himself adequately through language and internalizes symbols and images. In the early adolescent period he develops the ability for conceptual learning. He can reason, he can doubt, he can argue with clarity and with ease. His inquiring mind has a hierarchy of values and their relative significance in his own life. He observes, examines, and reflects on facts, and forms his own conclusions. The pupil's need to be personally involved in his own learning persists all through his life.

Educators inform us that children learn approximately:

> 10% of what they hear
> 20% of what they read
> 50% of what they see
> 90% of what they do

This makes it imperative that the teacher plan so that the child has the maximum opportunity to be personally responsible for his learning.

Children learn by exposure and dialogue. The chief duty of the teacher is to expose the students to a variety of experiences and resources for interest stimulation. A concert, a trip to a museum, a display of art and artifacts in the classroom, books, maps, audiovisual aids, resource persons—all provide impressions that motivate the child's expression.

Great music, great literature, creative acts, moments of courage from the lives of great men of history heighten the pupil's emotions. His perception of what is significant to him needs to be shared. The teacher, conscious of this moment of readiness, provides the opportunity for genuine sharing. In a climate of mutual trust this experience becomes sheer delight. Discussion, writing, painting, modeling, creative movement, composing music are all desirable forms of expression. Each achievement, each effort, will be valued as a labor of love.

Children learn by problem-solving. This is the best method of learning. Teachers can think of various situations of anxiety or inner tension in which children might be involved at home, in school, or in the community. Children can role-play the situations or freely discuss the problem, and give a variety of suggestions for solutions. The group can then decide what solution is best.

Mr. Smith used this method extensively because he believed in its effect. "Who has a problem?" he would ask as he looked at each child like a loving and concerned father. Frank was having a problem with Sam, a boy in the neighborhood who bullied him and ordered him around. After some discussion the class understood the seriousness of the problem and eagerly offered some valuable solutions. Then Mark, with a look of inner knowing, said, "If you want me to go with you to Sam's house I will be glad to go. I think he should know how you feel way inside." The class agreed this was a fine solution. On Monday after school Frank and Mark went to Sam's home.

Children learn by meaningful memorization. Frequent, well-planned repetition reinforces the learning of hymns, poems, prose, figures. The child retains more when the subject matter is life-centered, exciting, and satisfying. He memorizes when the material is used often in meaningful situations.

Good poetry, like good music, flows. It touches the inner strings of the heart. Its rhythm, its beauty, the depth of the concepts, the relevance of its intent to the reality concept of the learner capture his imagination and penetrate into his inner being. Great ideas then are made sacred possessions and are available whenever the person is ready for recall. Thomas Fuller defined memory as "the treasure-house of the mind wherein the monuments thereof are kept and preserved." Wordsworth called memory "the inward eye." A child defined it as "the things that I forget with."[2]

There has been a trend in education to negate the usefulness of storing facts in the mind through memorization because its value has been restricted to the child's definition. Unfortunately, in the past, memory work has been advocated for the sake of establishing a person's religiosity. Children were able to parrot words, often without understanding their sense or seeing any relationship between the subject matter learned and its application in day-to-day living. It was a duty to perform. This, however, should not blind the teacher of today to the place meaningful memorization can have in a learning situation. A rich memory sustains, inspires, and uplifts.

Memorization inscribes and engraves meanings on the mind. Great care should be taken to choose hymns and Bible passages that are worthy of memorization. A discussion on the background or the context of the material and its implications is invaluable in stimulating and enhancing learning.

FACTORS IN LEARNING

Annoyance. A conscientious teacher misses her children when they are absent. At the supermarket or the bank or on the telephone, the conversation goes something like this:

Teacher: Good morning, Mrs. Indifferent. This is Mrs. Eager. I missed Peter on Sunday. Is he sick? I'd like to send a card if he is.

---

[2] *Roget's International Thesaurus* (3d ed.; New York: Thomas Y. Crowell Co., 1962), 535:2.

Parent: No. He's not sick, Mrs. Eager. Frankly, he is bored in Sunday school. He says everyone is fooling around and he doesn't even hear what you are saying.

Teacher: That's too bad. The noise is creative noise.

Everyone is happily engaged in some purposeful activity. An atmosphere of bustling activity may annoy a child who is accustomed to work in quiet concentration. Boredom is sometimes the cause of a child's absence. He may see no novelty in the situation. Perhaps he finds the characters in stories either too naïve or too unreachable and is unable to identify himself with any situation. There may be other problems that a teacher fails to observe, such as tension and lack of harmony or some rejection of a boy or girl, verbally or in attitude. Sometimes a teacher's approach is not very inviting. He may favor one child—perhaps unintentionally—but children are very sensitive to unfair treatment. Sarcasm, aloofness, and sentimental affection can be very annoying and embarrassing to the child. The embarrassment of one child can embarrass all children and affect learning.

Level of aspiration. This is the goal set by the child himself for his performance. He experiences success or failure in terms of his own past or the standards set by his group or teacher. If the standards set for him are reachable, he will henceforth set realistic goals for himself. It is possible that he expresses a high level of aspiration to please the teacher while in reality his performance is very low. It is important, therefore, to try to know what the child's goals really are.

There has been limited research in this area. The general conclusion is that individuals who have successful experiences in a task area tend to have fairly realistic levels of aspiration—success usually leads to success. But failure does not *necessarily* lead to failure. The implication for the teacher is that a success orientation seems to be a more effective atmosphere. The insecure child feels defeated when he fails; he is hurt and loses a great deal of self-respect: "I can't do anything well. I failed again." He needs to be guided and encouraged to try again and again until he has gained some sense of success. The secure child takes defeat more gracefully; he feels challenged and tries again.

Psychological readiness or maturation. Maturation is a ripening process. Increased physical growth increases a child's capacity to learn and his readiness to profit from experiences. As his skills grow, he moves from simple to more complex patterns. All learning requires a degree of aptitude; for more difficult material a higher degree of aptitude is required. It is unwise to demand performances beyond a child's psychological reach. The child matures at his own pace. But a culturally rich environment nourishes and advances readiness for learning and a poor environment can slow mental growth or bring it to a halt.

A felt need. The child is usually aware of his own area of concern and anxiety. He may not wish or be able to communicate this need to his teacher, but his behavior shows that he is looking for an answer and reaching out for help.

Teachers often assume that they understand children's needs and they present platitudes: "Be a good boy; God wants you to be a good boy." This may sound impressive to a teacher, but it is absurd to a child. He is looking for a specific remedy. If during three or four Sundays he finds no help, he will feel restless, and everyone else will suffer with him. The inner child is never reached by platitudes, imposed rules, or force, but by warmth and acceptance.

Recognition and praise. Fear of punishment or fear in a given situation can accelerate a child's motivation for learning. He will muster all his energy to meet the emergency. The effect of stress, however, varies with individuals. For some it can become a strong motivating force while for others it can create emotional blocks which will damage learning. Punishment, if necessary at all, must be used wisely and sparingly. The child will learn more from his little successes and will more readily respond to recognition and praise, especially when it comes from people he loves and admires. He will learn least of all when he is ignored.

Competition and cooperation. Psychologists say that competition is learned rather than inborn. Most children learn faster through competition than cooperation because it provides the incentive to call forth undivided attention to improve and excel. The pursuit of excellence requires discipline, hard work, and good study habits. Competition needs constructive handling because it can become an obsession with the pupil. The unfortunate effects of competition can be avoided if the goals set up are attainable and the rules of fair play are observed and valued by all participants. A variety of methods have been used to lessen the undesirable effects of competition; one method is to rank the pupil with other learners in terms of the improvement he makes— the poor performer is given the chance to compete with his past performance and win.

Cooperation in working on a common project for a common good also is rewarding since a child is basically a social being. Each child can have equal opportunity in making contributions in the area of his interest and strength. A healthy interchange of ideas and interaction among learners can be a very potent force in bringing about behavior change. Cooperation requires careful handling too, lest it lead to mediocre performance.

Both cooperation and competition are essential for growth because both are common and true to life.

Motivation. No learning or change in behavior takes place unmotivated, whether it is learning of content, skills, or basic values and attitudes. Learning is advanced by the child's intent to learn.

This concept cannot be discussed apart from the motives of the teacher. His personal enthusiasm, knowledge, ability to listen and to communicate his faith—all enhance the child's desire to learn.

Incentive for learning also comes from an interest in the activities themselves. It is difficult to interest a child in learning what is out of date. "Points of contact have to be created with the present and existing interest, and the range of interests has to be expanded, whether children or adults are learning."[3]

However, it would be false for the teacher to think that the child's motives must limit what he will learn. The child's interests, important as they are, cannot determine content. If this were so, the teacher would be merely a disinterested bystander. The child's motivation can be heightened or intensified, influenced and charged to action by a responsible educator who understands his learning objectives and communicates this fact clearly to the child.

The climate for learning. The teacher who believes that knowledge is not absolute but open-ended will consciously plan an environment which will stimulate inquiry, interaction, and the use of a variety of talents. He will provide problems and challenges that appeal to different students. The room can be vibrant with enthusiasm as each student helps himself to available resources and gathers his data and information in his area of interest. The search for the unknown is always frustrating. There will be hardships along the way. The teacher, aware of the student's fears, will try to free him from his despair. He will strengthen his self-confidence so he can plunge once again into his search. The pupil's intellectual growth, the consciousness that the mastery of a skill has opened doors into the inquiry of broader subjects, gives him a deepening sense of inner satisfaction. He also finds it rewarding to know that he can count on his peers for help. He is

---

[3] Perry LeFevre, "Insights into Psychology for Christian Teachers," an address delivered at a meeting of the church school staff of First Congregational Church, Western Springs, Illinois.

grateful for the expression of genuine feelings, constructive criticism, as each person checks, tests, and evaluates his findings. Each pupil in his own way is learning to become a producer of ideas and information rather than a consumer. The environment that optimizes learning, that creates a respect and love for the cultivation of human values, puts the student on the road to mature self-direction.

Relationship with the teacher. In schools where teaching machines are extensively used, the children appear interested and excited. A child engaged in multiplication or spelling discovers at once whether his answer is correct; reinforcement or reward comes immediately for adequate performance. But the teacher is there too; he moves from desk to desk, guiding, correcting, instructing, and answering questions. Machines, no matter how good, can never replace a mature and loving teacher. A teaching-learning situation demands person-to-person encounter, honesty in communication, and openness in sharing the inner self. The teacher's love of the child, his sensitivity to his needs, his joy in teaching, his positive attitude toward life cannot fail to stir up imagination and make the child want to find meaning and direction for his life. This involves much more than knowledge of Bible verses, creeds, or a set of beliefs which he can articulate with ease. Potent ideas and personal example can transform life if a pupil has respect and love for the person who leads the way.

This is just what happened to Jesus' disciples. They found a man, a teacher, through whom they encountered God. Their response to God and to their fellowmen developed and matured through this one-to-one relationship with their teacher. In this relationship each one found not only his actual self but his possible self.

Chapter Four

Teachers Do Not Come Ready-made

If you are sure that you are a guide to the blind, a light to those who are in darkness, a corrector of the foolish, a teacher of children, having in the law the embodiment of knowledge and truth— you then who teach others, will you not teach yourself? —ROMANS 2:19-21

THE TEACHER'S PERSONAL PLAN

Mrs. Bored opened her closet on Sunday morning, five minutes before class time, and looked up and down the shelves. With no apology in her voice she said, "Let me see, what shall I teach this morning?" She had no song in her heart and she failed to see the glow on the faces of the happy children. She denied herself the joy of being fired by a noble purpose and the joy of doing something worthwhile. Needless to say, such indifference toward children is shocking and insulting to the Christian belief in the worth of each child.

Good teaching is planned teaching. A teacher needs to know his goals and his subject matter; he needs to know where he is going and how to get there. Most church school teachers seek the *how* before the *why,* for they feel this is the most urgent need; but this approach lacks conviction and enthusiasm.

Each unit and session of the teacher's manual is thoughtfully planned; but despite this wonderful plan, teaching can be hap- hazard. Therefore, in planning his lessons, the teacher should read carefully and thoughtfully the introduction and table of contents of his text and preview the whole unit, noting the objec- tive, familiarizing himself with the content and appropriate methods, and considering the needs of each child.

In planning the lesson he can underline key ideas and words. For further information he will consult *The Interpreter's Bible,* a Bible dictionary, or an encyclopedia. A written lesson plan will be very useful.

The teacher plans his lesson early in the week so that ideas will mature in his mind. During the rest of the week he will be alert to additional information in newspapers, journals, and TV pro- grams and will appropriate whatever may be useful. On Sunday morning he will have everything in readiness in his room and will be relaxed and ready to greet early arrivals. *Spontaneity comes after careful planning.*

YARDSTICKS FOR SELF-APPRAISAL

I love Louise because she is so cute and Marjorie because she is so creative and Joe because he is so much fun. But, oh, what shall I do with Martha?

What teacher has not asked himself such a question?

Good teaching requires honest self-appraisal. A program is judged on the basis of the quality of its objectives, goals, design, content, relationships (between teacher and pupil and among pupils themselves), and the climate for learning.

Objectives. The teacher needs to have an objective to deter- mine the direction of his plan and give significance to its components. It is important to distinguish between long- and short-range goals. For long-range objectives he can afford to be more idealistic; for individual sessions, more realistic, down-to-earth goals are necessary. It is well to write down the objective. The teacher can then look at it, reflect upon it, and raise questions in his mind as to its validity.

In evaluating each session the teacher accepts, tolerates, or condemns in relation to the goals he has set. He may be in despair or feel frustration, and this is a good tonic; but the questions that must be asked are: Is the objective possible? Are the expectations realistic? He may find that the class session does not follow the lesson plan; this need not disturb him. He should be flexible and allow room for children's questions where interest is shown.

Design. A program to be functional must have a design, a plan, a framework, based on the children's needs. Each Sunday session is part of the total design, and the teacher should time each activity as precisely as he can. He needs to ask, "Did I overplan and rush the children breathlessly from one activity to another? Did I underplan, causing boredom and restlessness? Did the children have any part in the planning? Did they feel it was their room, their activity, their purpose, as well as mine?"

Content. The content includes stories, discussion, questions, activities, Bible references, worship. It is wise for the teacher to follow the recommendations prescribed in the curriculum. Each session is thought through carefully in terms of its theological concepts, its relevance to the child's experience, the interest level of the activities and their meaning for him. Stories and Bible references are selected which have élan vital (life force) for today.

A well-planned curriculum does not stifle or curb creativity; it opens doors for personal spontaneity and enrichment. The teacher needs to ask himself questions such as these: Was the content based on the child's vital need? Was it adapted to his developing abilities? Did I challenge his thinking? Did I do more pouring in than drawing out? Did I ask him, "What do you think?" Was I specific enough to plan for the needs of individual children?

Relationships. Mature and loving relationships inside and outside the classroom offer the teacher his key to success. He will ask himself: Did all the children participate? Did they appear satisfied? moody? indifferent? Why? Was I relaxed, or nervous? Who was absent? Shall I call or send a card? How can I make Laura feel she is an important member of the class?

Some of these questions will be answered for the teacher if the sessions are recorded on tape for two or three Sundays in a row. In listening to himself and the children, the teacher will be amazed at the insights he gains.

A survey was made in a church school to find out what children thought and felt about their teachers. The children ranged in age from four to sixteen. These responses were included:

I like my teacher because she smiles . . . is enthusiastic and interesting . . . has a pleasant voice.

I like teachers who have lots of things to talk about . . . who don't beat around the bush in giving answers . . . who are open-minded . . . who make lessons fun and interesting.

I like my teacher because she hugs me . . . because she likes me . . . because she has no pets.

I like teachers who take disciplinary action when necessary . . . who have a sense of humor . . . who are considerate, who listen to the pupils.

My teacher is my mother away from my mother who helps me with my problems.

I appreciate a teacher who will reason out a point of contention even though the teacher and pupil have different points of view.

I like teachers who do not ridicule mistakes but make corrections in a constructive way.

I like my teacher because she doesn't yell at me.

How does the teacher rate himself in terms of these standards? Most of the statements refer to personal relationships. The pupil wants to be loved and understood, to be heard, to feel comfortable; he wants kindness, fairness, respect—just as adults do, only a child's need is often more desperate and urgent.

THE CONTAGION OF GROUP LEARNING

Some teachers like to do their own thinking and learning. Others feel the need to be exposed to and strengthened by the thoughts and skills of trained and experienced leaders. Many local churches meet this need by departmental and staff meetings. This is especially true where there is a director of Christian education or a minister who is vitally concerned with the Christian growth of young people. Sometimes churches cooperate with area workshops and laboratory schools. Teachers who really want to become more effective and inspiring should plan to take advantage of these opportunities.

Departmental meetings. In large churches where there are several teachers in each grade it is important that they gather once a month to share in planning lessons. Good work can be accomplished with a deep sense of fellowship when teachers meet in one another's homes over a cup of coffee. It is imperative that each teacher read his lessons and do as much personal planning as possible before the meeting.

The lead teacher or the departmental superintendent plays a key role. He acts as an administrator, educator, and counselor. He administers and organizes his department. He discovers the needs of his teachers for supplies, space, equipment, additional resources, and resource people. He makes these needs known to the general superintendent and/or the director of Christian education. He calls his teachers once a month or so to a departmental meeting.

He seeks to grow in his understanding of the philosophy of education, the theology underlying the curriculum, the skills and methods necessary for effective teaching. He communicates his understanding and learning to his teachers. He provides in-service training for his new teachers and guides them in their work. He encourages all his teachers to attend the local and area teacher-training workshops and accompanies them.

He encourages an honest sharing of problems and interchange of ideas and recommendations for improvements. He listens patiently and with understanding to all grievances and is sympathetic about problems. His dedication and vitality strikes a similar chord in his teachers. He is a minister to his ministers. And teachers find it a joy to work with him.

At a departmental meeting teachers need to discuss and suggest solutions for administrative problems. These might include absenteeism, substitute teachers, tardiness of teachers, use of supplies, stewardship, teacher-parent relationships.

Staff meetings. After returning from outer space, Lt. Col. John Glenn said:

> Exploration and the pursuit of knowledge have always paid dividends in the long run, usually far greater than anything expected at the outset. Knowledge begets knowledge. The more I see, the more I am impressed—not with how much we know, but with how tremendous the areas are that are as yet unexplored.[1]

Learned people are continually humbled by what they do not know. Their holy curiosity, their search for truth, and their experimental approach to existence give them eminence, inner

---

[1] In an address to a joint session of Congress, February 26, 1962.

beauty, and dignity. The self-satisfied man vanishes into gradual insignificance because he suffers from lack of mental and spiritual nourishment.

Staff meetings for all church school teachers are planned with the specific purpose of adding depth dimension to the already existing, vague, unrooted concepts they hold. Discussions are not intended to satisfy the needs of individuals for the following Sunday sessions; their ultimate purpose is to help teachers to discover and to develop a personal faith worthy of being communicated to children. Topics such as these might be used at meetings: Jesus in Our Contemporary World, History of the Early Christian Church, It Matters What You Believe.

Staff meetings are planned for about two hours, with a variety of methods of presentation—lecture and discussion, panel, buzz groups, film, workshop. Each session is planned to help teachers discover the relationship between theory and practice, and to enable them to make decisions on the basis of long-range rather than immediate goals.

Area workshops. "You have given me courage to go on." "I can hardly express my appreciation." "My own Christian education was pretty inadequate and my faith pretty shallow." Comments like these pour from teachers at the close of a workshop. Each in his own way meets God and feels his presence in the deep relationships. Workshops are planned to preview the curriculum, to increase skill in using the tools of teaching. Teachers wrestle with ideas and work in educational activities.

Laboratory schools. Demonstration schools are planned for one or two weeks. Children are taught by the counseling teacher and assistant student teachers. Lessons are planned cooperatively and each session is followed by appraisal. The counseling teacher is not exempt from criticism but invites comments and suggestions. Each teacher volunteers or is guided to take his turn telling stories, leading discussions, planning and leading worship services, and preparing and leading activities. These excerpts from student teachers' evaluations suggest the worth of these sessions: "It has given me more confidence in myself as a teacher." "I gained the most help in the evaluation and discussion periods. To find out how things are done and problems solved in other church schools has been most beneficial to me." "Meeting so many men and women devoted to the Christian training of our youth was a thrill to me." "Through the lives of our associates we found a stimulating experience of Christian faith."

If the teacher is to be "a guide to the blind, a light to those who are in darkness, a corrector of the foolish," then he will want to be involved in planned training sessions to be enlightened and enriched through exposure and nurture. *Good teachers do not come ready-made.*

Team teaching. In team teaching two or more teachers with specialized training, skills, aptitudes, and interests work together with the same group of children. They plan together, exchange ideas, evaluate approaches and support each other's contributions. Team teaching does not necessarily imply regrouping of pupils, though this may be necessary occasionally when pupils of similar interests and abilities wish to work on the same project. Each teacher contributes to the total program in the area where he excels and feels confident. There is no hierarchy here, no prima donna. The maximum opportunity is provided for learning both for the teachers and the children as each person satisfies his own needs and grows in knowledge and skills in the areas of his own lesser aptitudes.

Team teaching works best among equals in ability and training. This is difficult in a church school where often one person is more experienced or better qualified than the rest. There can be a period of creative conflict in the initial working stages when teachers are getting acquainted with each other's special interests and discovering their own concept about the art and science of teaching. There may be arguments and disagreements, but where there is love and maturity, there will be acceptance and understanding of the differences. Flexibility, objectivity, willingness to listen and to accept change or live with the status quo if necessary are all essential.

Bringing order out of chaos takes planning; good work cannot grow out of poor planning. The team will need a leader to initiate the first move. After that, members will draw out each other's unique and special contributions.

Planning sessions should always include evaluation. Even constructive criticism may appear harsh to the one involved, but all teachers need to upgrade their teaching techniques so as to equip themselves for the teaching ministry.

A division of labor with delegation of responsibility and the authority to make decisions does not weaken the program but actually strengthens it.

There is no shortcut to good teaching. It demands concentrated and disciplined effort and, above all, dedication. Despite all his planning and his love for the children, the teacher may not leave every session glowing. Some seeds fall on rocks. There is apathy. There are problems and frustrations. But as W. E. Hocking says, "There *is no costless* comfort to be had in this world, still less a costless joy. For there is no satisfaction of the will apart from work done—in the end, of taking a share in world-making. . . . Not even love can come to its own without pain."[2]

---

[2] William Ernest Hocking, *The Coming World Civilization* (New York: Harper & Bros., 1956), p. 164.

Chapter Five

Creative Teaching

The artist's unique gift is to see beyond the narrow reality of the moment into the breadth of eternity.[1]

—KATHARINE MORRISON MC CLINTON

THE CREATIVE APPROACH

Mrs. Norman stood at the door and welcomed each child coming to the first session of the church school. The juniors were fascinated by what they saw. There were maps and flat pictures on bulletin boards. Attractive books, opened to pictures dealing with the unit of study, were displayed on low tables. There were open Bibles in different translations and art and artifacts from Jordan and Israel. The children wandered among these displays, feeding their eyes and minds. They were allowed to touch and feel. Each child was to report to his group about one or two items especially interesting to him. Then the teacher introduced the unit of study: the lives of four minor prophets—Amos, Hosea, Micah, Joel.

---

[1] Katharine Morrison McClinton, *Christian Church Art Through the Ages* (New York: Macmillan, 1962), p. 1.

After some discussion the students decided to divide into various interest groups. Some boys chose to draw a map to indicate the towns where each of these prophets had lived, and they studied the topography and climate of the land. Several girls chose to work on a mural to give a biographical sketch of the prophets in picture and words. The whole group wrote a script showing how each of the prophets denounced the corruption in his society and telling of his unique contribution to the religion of Israel. A third interest group depicted the corruption in present-day society through role-playing and then discussed possible solutions, searching the Christian faith for help in solving contemporary problems. The children brought newspaper clippings that showed evidence of corruption in their society and talked about what they could do or what different organizations were already doing to meet these problems.

The teacher gave each group the necessary guidance and references both from the Bible and other resource books; then they were on their own. When additional help was needed, the children raised their hands. Naturally this project took several Sundays and one or two weekday afternoons for taping the script. No one complained of boredom. From the very start there was two-way communication. The juniors were exposed to ideas, but ideas were not imposed on them; they were invited to participate in an experience that was purposeful and interesting to them. Music, worship, scripture-reading—all planned with the children—broadened and deepened their knowledge.

Children enjoy projects because for them this is the *real thing*. As they share supplies, discuss ideas, observe finished projects, they grow in their own sense of worth as well as in their respect for each other's achievement. Each child brings to his task something of himself, and his mind is fired to generate new concepts and approaches. He finds freedom that enables him to become more flexible, receptive, and experimental.

Unfortunately many church school teachers fail to see teaching in this light. Some are dubious about the value of the creative approach insisting on the traditional pattern which, however, is monotonous because it lacks novelty and variety which motivate and interest the learner and give him a sense of purpose. When the teacher works only in his own cherished way, the child finds himself in a strange land listening to a foreign language.

Other teachers believe in the creative process but do not know how to go about it; they lack technical skills. They are unable to break through the traditional concept of several small continuous classes working independently, joining together for worship led by a superintendent or lead teacher. They are fearful of the project method: "What are those children doing while I'm working with these? What about children who finish before others are done? How do I organize my classroom when different groups are doing different things at the same time?"

Technical skills can be learned in area workshops or local churches under skilled technicians who may be found among parents or public schoolteachers who would be happy to help out for a few Sunday mornings.

The teacher is constantly surprised by joy as he grows in understanding and appreciation of the intrinsic value of creative teaching. He observes the intense aliveness of a pupil, a child's joy in working with other children, a grateful response to his teaching. Teaching becomes a blessing he had not counted on and this brightens his day and unveils a hidden joy.

Imagination is the key to creativity. Often it is more important than knowledge. Imagination is the tool every creative teacher uses to enlarge the child's vision and to help him listen to himself and respond to the voice from within. Jerome S. Bruner defines creativity as "effective surprise—the production of novelty." He affirms that the creative person is willing to divorce himself from the obvious forms as they exist. While he detaches himself from the combination of the previous ideas he commits himself to the discovery of new forms and patterns for expression. "For there is about it a caring, a deep need to understand something, to master a technique, to rerender a meaning."[2] In the child's early years, the teacher concentrates on the working process that leads to wholeness rather than the quality of the finished product. With increasing maturity the child will want to pursue excellence and create a product worthy of his respect.

The curricula of most denominations are centered around three major themes—the Bible, the life of Jesus, and church history. The following paragraphs are samplings of classroom experiences that creativity and imagination in teaching show in each of these areas.

TEACHING THE BIBLE

Children from the fourth through the eighth grades were studying the Bible. After a planning session they chose three projects: murals, to depict the contributions of the great personalities of the Bible from creation to Jesus; maps to locate the birthplace of each of these personalities; biographies to portray a short summary of the life of each of these people. All the groups did extensive research work from many sources made available to them. A fourth-grader worked with an eighth-grade child without embarrassment; they did not try to compete or conform because they had a mutual interest. Enthusiasm and interest mounted. As the children learned the hymn "For Man's Unceasing Quest for God" they expressed a desire to write their own words. Four children composed new words and another accompanied the whole group on his violin.

The high point of the entire experience was the sharing time. Murals, maps, and stories were all displayed and arranged in chronological order. Children moved from table to table examining each detail carefully and reading the stories. They sat in a

---

[2] Jerome S. Bruner, *On Knowing: Essays for the Left Hand* (Cambridge, Mass.: Harvard University Press, 1962), p. 24.

circle, and each child talked about his project, the resources he had used, and the weakness and strength of each personality studied. In a short time the wealth of one person became the common wealth.

The children decided to share their experiences with their parents and invited them to one pupil's spacious backyard. Teachers, parents, and children dressed in Palestinian costumes sat around the campfire listening to the story of each child and later examined the careful and detailed work displayed. For refreshments there were olives, cheese, figs, grapes, and matzos. The evening closed with everyone singing the new hymn words, accompanied by the violin.

This was an unforgettable experience for all the participants. Even several years later, looking back, they felt closely drawn to one another by the great ideas that had touched their lives, by God's loving concern for them and their own unceasing quest for him.

TEACHING THE LIFE OF JESUS

"No, not Jesus again," remarked one kindergarten child. But this was not the experience of twenty-five fourth-graders who for a whole year studied the life of Jesus. They discovered that Jesus was not a myth or a fictitious character, but a real person who lived and died to reveal God's eternal love to man.

The children worked in three different interest groups. The first group decided to study the biography of Jesus from birth to resurrection. The second chose to study the teachings of Jesus through his parables. The third studied the events in Passion Week, from Palm Sunday through the resurrection.

In the biography group each child was assigned two or three stories to be read from the Bible and various other books for clarification of ideas. The children told each other their stories in their own words before writing them down. These stories were put together in chronological order and mimeographed. Tape recordings were made of each child reading his story. The tape was played back, and after several rehearsals recorded again, to the great satisfaction of the listeners. Children, wearing colorful costumes, then played the characters in these stories. Their pictures were taken in colored slides. The children prepared large backdrops for these pictures, and whenever possible, went to the seashore, a hillside, or a field to give authenticity to the background. They borrowed a donkey to give color and realism to the Palm Sunday story of Jesus' entry into Jerusalem. Children from all interest groups took part in the visual presentation of the life of Jesus. Several wanted to depict Jesus and were allowed to do so. At the end of the long, exciting, and arduous project, a teacher who had taken the pictures and helped in the story-writing remarked, "I did not believe in all this, but I am convinced that this is a very effective and interesting way of teaching. Children were always there and interest was at its peak. No teacher can ask for more."

The teachings of Jesus through parables were made a study project through creative drama. The children prepared their stage with velvet drapes secured from church families. Paper-bag puppets were made by the children to help them play the characters they had chosen to be. Some preferred to dramatize the parables through costumes. Headgear alone often was enough to help them lose their self-consciousness. Parables were always read aloud first; then each child read quietly from his own Bible. Questions were asked and answered to clarify ideas. Scripts were written for some parables. Each performance was evaluated by the children in terms of the quality of communication of content, feeling, and realism. One child said, "I can hide behind this puppet and say what I please."

The mural group illustrated the events of Passion Week through pictures and stories. They used pastels, tempera paint, India ink, crayons, felt pens. They worked with great care and were proud of their achievements, feeling an almost sacramental value in them. They had entered into the life and thoughts of Jesus intimately and personally.

All the children looked forward to the sharing time. They decorated their room and worship center; then they sat in a circle and became the audience. The stories on the tape recorder and the slides were synchronized and projected on the screen. Children heard their voices and saw themselves portraying various characters in different stories. They lived the life of Jesus with Jesus. And then, since every joy needs to be shared, parents were invited to an open house to witness this great achievement.

To these children Jesus is and always will be alive. At Christmas they will go to the manger, bringing their gifts of love and gratitude for a life lived so fully and abundantly. On Palm Sunday they will sing their hosannas carrying their palm branches to Jerusalem. They will go to Golgotha and hear the words, "Father, forgive them; for they know not what they do." On Easter Sunday they will truly understand the meaning of the words, "Why do you seek the living among the dead? He is risen!"

TEACHING CHURCH HISTORY

Church history unfolds the past to guide the present. The study of history can be very meaningful if the learner feels there is a direct line of communication from the heroes of the past to his personal life. Much truth has been discovered by them and need not be rediscovered, for they have shown the peaks as well as the valleys. Theirs were lives of agony, shame, misery, fear; but also of hope, joy, and victory. There is an aliveness in their testimony: "I have been crucified with Christ; it is no longer I who live, but Christ who lives in me; and the life I now live in the flesh I live by faith in the Son of God who loved me and gave himself for me" (Gal. 2:20).

Church history begins with the book of Acts and continues through the book of Revelation right up to the present day. It discloses the lives of men and women who were nurtured by the word of God; they claim no honor or glory for their heroic acts but attribute them to the power of God working in and through them.

Creative teaching is especially essential in church history. Many teachers find it difficult to get excited about this subject; they say it fails to use the Bible and is of less meaning and value. They are unable to be challenged by the vigor and spiritual power of these men. Children find it hard to get excited about Augustine or Benedict of Nursia, heresies or the Reformation.

One group of junior highs grew enthusiastic about the life of Martin Luther when their teacher wrote a simple script in the style of the television program "This Is Your Life." As the children listened or took part in acting out the script, they warmed up to the whole idea. The teacher invited them to her home for further rehearsal and discussion. Over hot chocolate they again read their parts and raised questions. They planned for props. They devised a gadget that would serve as an airplane and would bring Luther to earth. Other classes were invited to the finished performance. Martin Luther had become a real person to the junior high class.

Such ideas may not be original with us teachers, but whether we find them in our curriculum materials, in a church-related magazine, or on the television screen, the important thing is to try them. They do work. And the joy we put into them and the joy we receive will keep them from being "too much work."

The study of Martin Luther was successful because it involved all the children in areas of their own particular interest. Activities provide the necessary tools to accelerate children's motivation to learn. The children should be encouraged to experiment and test different materials to give them the assurance that the means which they choose provide the best vehicle for their own expression. Children with similar interests share their insights, knowledge, and skills. Individual expression ultimately becomes group expression. In a short span of time children cover more ground in terms of content—facts, figures, concepts—with great interest and understanding. But above all a close fellowship develops among the participants.

SOME RECOMMENDED ACTIVITIES

Storytelling. The teacher told a story about a lonely child—the one with whom no one liked to play. He was crude and loud; he felt hurt and bitter inside; so he hit other boys and girls. The story was a tool to reach three aggressive boys; the teacher hoped that if he dramatized the agony and the despair, they might be able to identify with the rejected boy. The story emphasized that although his teacher disapproved of his behavior, he loved the child because he saw in him great potential for good. The story made the point; the boys consciously tried to be kind, thoughtful, and courteous.

Storytelling is a creative art. The teacher projects through words his feelings, his ideals, his realistic expectations, in a manner that inspires and enriches the listener. He can do this only if the chosen story is real to him and to the children and if they can understand how the characters feel.

A story can be told simply and naturally. Its message will be woven into the fabric of words, not left as an appendix at the end of the story—"And the moral is. . . ." The story that carries the power of convictions is alive. A teacher may spend hours discarding one story after another because the message does not ring true. He can always write his own, or improvise on a story he likes in part. He will find that children are a rich resource for stories; he will watch them carefully and become acquainted with their concerns and hurts, and their world. He will watch newspapers, study history, and above all use the stories Jesus told. The stories show God's abiding love for each person, reaching out to seek and to save the lost and the unlovely—the prodigal son, the lost sheep, the owner of the vineyard, Zacchaeus. These stories have greater significance for the teacher if he uses *The Interpreter's Bible* for clarification of meanings. The teacher will tell the story in his own words; then he will read the same story from the Bible. If he is not a "born" storyteller he can learn to become one.

Dramatics. "Dramatics" refers to the portrayal of ideas and events of a story by amateur actors. It has a tremendous potential for teaching and is now widely used in many church schools where the emphasis is on self-discovery through self-expression.

The chosen story, such as the parable of the talents in Matthew 25:14-30 will have a message, action, and dialogue. The players will feel and understand the emotion of their characters. They will think their thoughts and communicate vividly to the audience. Players who can identify themselves with their characters usually evoke a response in themselves as well as in those with whom they share their experience. They think consciously or unconsciously about questions such as: What is this life all about? What role do I play on this stage of life? What will be the outcome?

Shy children should be encouraged by the teacher's smile and touch to participate. If they prefer to be spectators they can be given other responsibilities. They can plan for props, costumes, backdrops. Doors for self-evaluation have been opened wide, not in terms of how well the children acted but of individuals wrestling with fundamental questions: What do I do with the talent I have? In what sense am I a steward of this incredible potential that I have? Am I accountable to anyone?

Some children are reluctant to speak before a group but can

be free and expressive in pantomime. All children and especially shy ones enjoy acting through the use of dolls, toy telephones, television screen, shadow theater. They hide behind these gadgets and lose their self-consciousness. Preschool children act out their feelings and experiences through papa and mama, sister and brother dolls. Toy telephones are used in upper as well as lower grades with children who have difficulty in expressing themselves in person-to-person relationships. Puppets are loved by all age-groups.

Role-playing. Stories for role-playing come from real life—interpersonal crises and conflicts. The story merely states the situation; it is a half-written story that needs no ending. For successful role-playing there should be good rapport between the members of the group and the teacher so they can trust their feelings to each other. The teacher states the situation as clearly as he can.

Every Sunday Judy attended church school, but none of her friends spoke to her. All they said was "move over"; and she moved over to make room for Susan, the popular girl. When they divided into committees to plan for a basketball game in a nearby school gym and a potluck supper at the church afterward, Judy was ignored. When they went to the ball game, Judy was not there. When they went to church for supper, Judy was not there. Next Sunday morning, Judy was not there.

After the roles are acted out by the children, the other members of the class interrogate the actors and probe into their feelings. They consider such questions as: How did you feel when you ignored Judy? How would you feel if you were Judy?

The purpose of role-playing is not primarily individual or group therapy, but as the discussion continues it becomes therapeutic. Areas of anxiety, which could be felt but could not be communicated verbally, are now in the open. The children listen to each other and feel empathy within the group as different members identify themselves with various feelings and personal needs. There is now a close fellowship. Members make great strides in self-understanding and self-respect as they honestly seek a solution together. The teacher gains valuable insight into the potential of each member and the values in which the group believes.

Creative writing. Children can be given many opportunities to express their own thoughts and feelings through the use of words. The richer their experience, the easier is the creation of ideas. If the teacher wants to make this a group project, he can ask the children about an experience they have all had together. It might have been a trip to a fair, a visit to a farm, worship at a synagogue, a special holiday celebration, a birthday party, or a summary at the end of a unit. The teacher jots down ideas of children on a chalkboard and underlines key words. He will act only as the scribe, not the mastermind.

Children enjoy writing scripts for puppet shows and informal dramatizations. No work is a finished piece of art, and the teacher should not judge the outcome on the basis of adult standards. Nevertheless he can help children raise their standards; a sensitive teacher will know which child can raise his sights and which one has already done his best.

Audiovisual aids. Audiovisual aids—slides, filmstrips, movies, recordings, maps, flat pictures—when used wisely can become very important teaching tools. Because this is an excellent attention-getting device, it is often abused. Audiovisual aids should be related to the unit of study to enrich content, arouse curiosity, and open doors for further research. The teacher should plan for this activity as he would plan for any other.

The main purpose for the use of audiovisual aids is to heighten attention; learning can then be accelerated and ideas retained for a long time. Much joy goes out of teaching if equipment does not work and the teacher has not bothered to check before Sunday morning. If equipment is not in working condition, it should be reported to the chairman of the audiovisual committee. If the teacher does not have the necessary aids in his own church he could seek the assistance of his general denominational office. Its staff is always willing and ready to serve.

CHILDREN AND ART

In the beginning—God
  created
  form out of chaos,
    curves, angles, symmetry, design;
  color out of darkness,
    shades, hues, tints, blendings;
  sound out of the silences,
    rhythm, cadence, tone, harmonies;
  and man
    to inhabit form
    to see color
    to hear sound
    and to respond in love
    to meanings.
              —BETTY E. STONE[3]

Teacher: Paint for me a beautiful picture of Easter.
Pupil: Easter?
Teacher: Yes, Easter is just around the corner.

This request was made on a cold day in February, and Easter was in the middle of April. The primary children had had no

---

[3] Betty E. Stone, "In the Beginning—God," *Children's Religion,* May, 1964, p. 2. Copyright, 1964, United Church Press.

previous discussion on Easter. They looked at each other, puzzled. They scribbled a few lines, toyed with crayons, and then simply looked bored. The teacher paid no attention to their work and asked no questions about their finished products. Her objective was to keep them busy so that she could plan her worship service.

The child's mind should be enriched by experiences in which he can fully participate. Buildup sessions through discussion, interviews, trips to art galleries, reading poetry or prose will fill his eyes, stir his imagination, and enhance his urge to spill out his love on the selected materials made available to him and best suited for his age. The teacher's own sensitivity to the needs of the child, his enthusiasm, his flexibility will create the rapport necessary to induce creativity. The child can paint and *will* paint in his unique way when he is allowed and encouraged to be experimental. The teacher's faith in his innate ability will evoke faith.

"I can't make a mistake," said a first-grade child. "I have to do it all over again."

"We all make mistakes," said the teacher.

"But I can't!" cried the little girl.

The five-year-old drew houses with windows and doors. The teacher put a chimney on each house with smoke ascending to the sky. The child picked up his picture, crumpled it, and threw it into the wastebasket.

"I can't draw a man," cried a little boy.

"Look at me," said the teacher. "What do you see?"

"I see two eyes, nose, lips . . ."

"Fine. Draw what you see."

These classroom situations point up the fact that when adult standards are forced on the child, he mistrusts his creative powers.

He is afraid to make mistakes. When adults intrude into the privacy of the child, he resents it and wants to destroy his creation. Art should be something *friendly* to each child through which he can communicate his fears, frustrations, hopes, and joys in symbolic language. Sensitive and informed teachers will understand the power of this friendship and encourage the child to wake up his dormant potential.

Viktor Lowenfeld's *Creative and Mental Growth*[4] is must-reading for all church school teachers, a profound, stimulating, and inspiring book—one of the best on art education. The author treats his subject from the developmental point of view. He says that the child's mental and creative growth are interdependent and that awareness of these different growth stages can help the teacher to understand and appreciate the child's creation.

The characteristics attributed to different age levels are not arbitrary but broad generalizations. Teachers will be aware that children develop at different speeds—and that those who are keenly interested in art and are also gifted develop faster.

Scribbling stage (ages 2-4). The two-year-old is interested in moving his hands and arms just to make a mark. With increasing development of his muscles, his movements become more controlled and free to make circular, vertical, or horizontal lines. He enjoys scribbling because he can move his lines as he pleases.

At three years, the child tells a story as he scribbles. This is his play activity. With further development, he becomes more conscious of his immediate family and scribbles a vivid family experience. He sets out to make the head of a person with a circular movement, adding eyes, nose, mouth, which partially indicate features. He is unable to express visually his mental image, but

---

[4] See Viktor Lowenfeld and W. Lambert Brittain, *Creative and Mental Growth* (4th ed.; New York: Macmillan, 1964). The author is indebted to Professor Lowenfeld for the names of the growth stages and for some of the ideas included in the following paragraphs.

this does not discourage him. Adults should show appreciation of his endeavor. It is unwise to ask, "Is that a dog? house? mother?" Instead, the adult can say, "I like your picture," in a tone of assurance. "Tell me about it." The child needs to work with materials suited to his age in size and quantity; they should be easy to manipulate—large, soft crayons; newsprint; malleable clay. He should be allowed to be messy in a corner set aside for messiness; a father's old shirt, turned backward and buttoned or pinned, makes a fine smock.

Preschematic stage (ages 4-7). The wider experiences of the child in his family, school, and playground provide him with vivid ideas, which are reflected in his drawing. Relationships between people and objects can be seen, features are well marked, and objects are well differentiated. The child will draw what is important to him and omit what is unessential. What appears essential today may not be essential tomorrow. He begins with an idea and changes it as he starts drawing. His attention span is very short, and he will tire soon.

Most children are free and spontaneous at this age. They enjoy the process of expression and are not particularly interested in adult reactions. If a child is afraid to draw, he probably has experienced some degree of adult scorn or criticism. The child looks for assurance, and he needs it.

Schematic stage (ages 7-9). The child achieves a definite form concept (schema) to illustrate a man, an animal, or an object, and he repeats this form in all his drawings. These symbols represent his mental image rather than his visual analysis of the man, his size, or the relation of the parts of his anatomy to each other. He may draw a large, circular head, a rectangular body smaller than the head, curved or straight single or double lines for arms and legs; he may add fingers and clothes.

Where there is a great discrepancy in his size relationships, he is definitely relating himself emotionally to his picture. An important fact is always exaggerated; an unimportant fact may be neglected or made very small. A starving child will draw a cookie larger than the jar that holds it.

A ground or base line is used—a horizontal line running along the bottom of the page around which the child organizes his people, trees, objects. This shows he has developed a feeling for space and environment and for the relationship of each of these objects to the other and to the environment. He feels a part of the environment, and this gives him a sense of security.

Color-consciousness also develops at this stage; the child sees a relation between color and object. This awakening gives him a sense of pride and a desire to explore further. He chooses the color he likes best and repeats it. He should be encouraged to try different colors; if repetition persists in every picture, it shows fear and rigidity.

Gang stage (ages 9-11). The child has a sense of identity and a feeling of power in his own group. He relates easily to his peers as well as to adults. He takes part in activities and shows this involvement and interaction in his pictures. He begins to draw his concept of people rather than their schema. He draws what appears real to him, which may or may not be the true likeness of his visual image. The intelligent child is very much aware of the changes in his environment and will use many variations and details in his drawings. He will show the horizon line, the sky; will be aware of depth, distance, proportion, difference in colors, texture, design.

Adults should satisfy the curiosity of the child by clarifying concepts for him, providing him with experiences to sharpen his awareness for all that is in his environment. He should be motivated to explore and experiment with a variety of techniques and materials to express himself in his own way.

Reasoning stage (ages 11-13). This is the transitional stage from childhood into adolescence. The child struggles for independence and is partially successful. He can handle most of his problems and he often asserts his individuality. But during the times of crisis he acts and feels like a child and is anxious for support and guidance. He is conscious of his physical development and his confusion is often expressed in the exaggeration of parts of the body. He has an acute sense of right and wrong, justice and injustice, honesty and lack of integrity. When adults or his peers violate his value standards, he finds an outlet in drawing distorted faces of people with exaggerated colors and the wrong shape and form of their bodies.

He is critical of his own world and his own creative product. He analyzes each picture carefully in terms of its intellectual, aesthetic, and emotional dimensions. He is aware now of optical effects—light and shadow, folds and wrinkles in a garment, motion, depth, distance. He is equally interested in the process of creating as in the product.

Children vary in their reactions to experiences. Some are visual-minded; others are nonvisual-minded. Both types need art stimulation through a model, discussion, or both. If they are to paint the story of the "unforgiving servant," they need to know who he is, where he lives, what he does, the people to whom he relates, how he feels.

The visual-minded child will form a realistic concept of his character from his visual impressions. He will have the whole picture in his mind, but like a spectator he will stand outside his picture looking in. He will adjust his colors to the object he is painting and will be conscious of perspective and an interpretation of space. He will insist on realism and accuracy. He will appreciate the product if it is an authentic duplicate of his visual impressions.

The nonvisual-minded child will create a subjective expression of his emotions and thoughts. He is a part of his picture and identifies with his characters. He will paint what is significant to him and delete details that seem less important or do not support his concept. He chooses the colors to which he can react emotionally even if they have no visual reference to the object. He is not interested in a pictorial description of an image. His purpose is to respond to his experience by unveiling his soul so his innermost needs are fulfilled.

Some children paint pictures that express a considerable amount of realism as well as personal emotional involvement. Teachers should understand these tendencies and encourage children to paint what they see and feel. Art can provide the best outlet for creative energies and can put the stamp of permanence on ideas.

The church school teacher does not need to be an art teacher, but it is important for him to be aware of what enhances and what inhibits creativity. These guidelines will be helpful:

- Accept the child's choice of form and medium of expression. Remember, there is no right or wrong in artistic expression. Freedom allows him to dare to be himself. Keep your hands off! If the child says, "Teacher, draw me a dog," say, "I like the way *you* draw it."
- Provide experiences. Remember the slogan "No expression without impression."
- Encourage the child to set his own standards. But raise or lower his level of aspiration when you find it unrealistic for him.
- Let the child paint at his own pace. Do not push.
- Encourage exploration and experimentation with different materials and techniques.
- Encourage individuality in self-expression; discourage imitative art.
- Allow the child to seek his standard of perfection, which will come with increasing maturity and self-discipline.
- Show your appreciation of the finished work by mounting it

or displaying it in a prominent place. This is the best motivation.

- Have a sharing time when each artist can give an outlet to his urge to communicate his experience. He is anxious to receive the response of the group. Give words of assurance that ring true to the child. He has opened a window and you can partially see his inner world. This is your moment of celebration.

Creative teachers are *artists*. They unlock doors to reveal the hidden glory in each creation. Artistic expression in all its forms—drama, music, dance, sculpture, painting, designing, writing—should be encouraged and promoted in all church schools. Every creation is an act of love, and every act of love is an expression of the divine-human encounter. The artist feels he is on holy ground; he feels the burning bush in his soul; he realizes more than ever his aliveness and sense of worth. His sensitivity to beauty and order, his sense of wonder and curiosity make him reach out for new dimensions in his life, thus fulfilling the will of the Creator when he first created man in his own image.

RESOURCES FOR CREATIVE ACTIVITIES[5]

Activities for Holidays	Keiser, *Here's How and When*, pp. 112-22 Rice, *Creative Activities*, chap. 4
Brainteasers	Keiser, *Here's How and When*, pp. 45-49
Clay Modeling	Cole, *The Arts in the Classroom*, chap. 2 Lobingier, *Activities in Child Education*, p. 124
Cornstarch Modeling	Keiser, *Here's How and When*, p. 151
Creative and Formal Drama Puppets—Script-writing— Role-playing—Radio and	Keiser, *Here's How and When*, chap. 3 Lobingier, *Activities in Child Education*, chap. 10

[5] See the Selected Bibliography, pp. 138 f., for full bibliographic details.

Television—Tape Recording—Use of Costumes—Taking Pictures—Shadow Pictures	Rice, *Creative Activities,* pp. 70, 99-102
Creative Writing Poem—Prayer—Litany	Cole, *Arts in the Classroom,* chap. 5 Keiser, *Here's How and When,* pp. 101 f. Rice, *Creative Activities,* pp. 14, 128
Diorama	Keiser, *Here's How and When,* pp. 25-30 Lobingier, *Activities in Child Education,* pp. 188, 190 Rice, *Creative Activities,* pp. 68-72
Frieze	Rice, *Creative Activities,* pp. 49 ff.
Maps	Keiser, *Here's How and When,* pp. 80 ff.
Movie	Keiser, *Here's How and When,* pp. 78 f.
Murals	Cole, *The Arts in the Classroom,* chap. 1 Keiser, *Here's How and When,* pp. 72 ff.
Papier-mâché Modeling	Keiser, *Here's How and When,* pp. 152, 156 Rice, *Creative Activities,* pp. 93 ff.
Peep Show	Keiser, *Here's How and When,* pp. 31 ff. Lobingier, *Activities in Child Education,* pp. 192 ff.
Time Line	Keiser, *Here's How and When,* pp. 82 f.
Trips	(Other churches and synagogues, centers of architecture and symbolism, exhibits of excavations, Bible exhibits)
Slides	Rice, *Creative Activities,* pp. 102-6

Chapter Six

The Lord High and Lifted Up

O Lord, our Lord,
how majestic is thy name in all the earth!
. . . .
When I look at thy heavens, the work of thy
fingers,
the moon and the stars which thou hast
established;
what is man that thou art mindful of him,
and the son of man that thou dost care for him?
Yet thou hast made him little less than God,
and dost crown him with glory and honor.

—PSALM 8:1, 3-5

WORSHIP AT THE CATACOMBS

"Have you seen a catacomb?" asked Laurie.

"Yes," I said, "one hot afternoon I found myself in the catacombs of Rome."

The class looked excited. "What is it like?" asked Larry.

The children and I had studied the life of Paul and the early Christians. We had emphasized their love and devotion to Jesus Christ, the risen Lord. We had talked about the early persecutions and how the Christians had sought refuge in the catacombs. Their need for corporate worship and fellowship had brought them together in this burial place many feet beneath the ground. I told the class how dark and humid the place had felt to me and how the many branching corridors seemed almost made as a hiding place for the worshipers. I could see ceilings of plaster and walls decorated with frescoes. There were religious subjects depicted through symbols. The catacombs were outside the city gates. Here the Christian martyrs were buried, and later other Christians. As the Christians gathered for worship they identified themselves with a password, a symbol known to them but unknown to non-Christians.

The children wanted to reenact one of these fellowship meetings. Spontaneous and creative ideas started pouring in. Each child made an oil lamp from clay and stuck a birthday candle in it. A dark room with bare floor was made to look like a catacomb. Two branches of a tree were stripped of their leaves and made into a rugged cross which was stuck into a clay base. The kitchen counter with the burning lamp and the cross became the altar.

Children and teachers, dressed in Palestinian costumes, came one by one to the door of the catacomb. One of the teachers stood at the door as a guard. Each child came with his lamp and gave his password: "Jesus of Nazareth," "Fish," "Jesus, the Son of God," "Jesus Christ, the risen Lord." He lit his lamp and went in and sat quietly on the bare floor facing the altar. The lighted candles in the dark room, the reflective mood of the children, their feeling of respect and awe—and then a voice would break the silence: "I remember the words of Jesus on the cross, 'Father, forgive them: for they know not what they do.'" Silence again; then: "I like best the story about Jesus, how he blessed little children and loved them." Each child or teacher shared one particular experience from the life of Jesus that had special meaning for him. Hymns were sung and then there was silence again. We all felt the presence of God and his love touching us, lifting us up from where we were to where we could see and know him in our minds and hearts. Tears fell on this holy ground. We felt drawn to each other; and we could sense how the early Christians must have felt toward one another as they worshiped together.

Much thought and group planning went into preparing the children for this experience. Minds had to be nourished, emotions had to be stirred up, the climate and mood had to be created.

CORPORATE WORSHIP

Corporate worship is as important as private worship. As a minister once put it, "There are some things we do best in fellowship." Jesus said, "Where two or three are gathered in my name, there am I in the midst of them" and "Pray . . . like this, Our Father. . . ." Worshipers come together with their common desires and needs for renewed strength to face the tides of life and to satisfy their need to offer themselves and their substance as a living sacrifice to God. Paul speaks about the priesthood of all believers who are embodied in Christ's church. They are called to carry out the responsibilities of a priest, to bring offerings to God—praise, adoration, glory to his name—to suffer vicariously for their fellowmen, bearing their pains and hurts, and offering intercessory prayers for the healing of one man and all men. Robert Weston, in his poem "A Man Could Stand Up," identifies himself with the anguish of humanity.

In times like these
It is easy to be dismayed
And easier still to shut one's eyes
To the tensions and turmoil of the world.
Too readily would I shut out
The conflict of nations and the clash of class with class,
The menace of human custom born in ignorance and darkness

Or insulated in protected comforts and wealth,
Deaf to the cry of the child
Going to bed hungry at night
Every night of its life.
It is painful to look out into the suffering world
And feel its responsibilities upon my shoulders.
What can one man do
Against the pressure of forces that seem steadily to mount
And are measured in millions of whatever units there be,
Whether work-hours or votes or bomb tons?
What can one man do?
He can stand up and be a man.
He can speak out and be heard.
He can be a voice as of "one crying in the wilderness."
There was one, once,
Who proved that a voice crying in the wilderness
Might change the pattern of the world.[1]

Both private and corporate worship prepare man for effective witness and service. If the love of one man for another is to survive, man must continue to worship God.

If "the chief end of man is to glorify God and enjoy him forever," as the Shorter Catechism declares, man needs to have the leisure to cultivate this awareness. Reflective and careful planning is necessary to nourish and quicken man's reach for this union.

PLANNED WORSHIP

Harold, a junior in college, prayed from the pulpit.

Father, you are not far away—not while there are little strawberries in the window there, not while you are so plain in the smiling face of a beloved friend. If we care to see, you are very near. Even the smallest leaf can sing your glory to

---

[1] Robert T. Weston, "A Man Could Stand Up," *Seasons of the Soul,* p. 17.

the heart that is open. You made us, Father, you gave us eyes to see and ears to hear and hair for the wind to blow and hearts that love and are loved and ache. . . . Let each of our hearts be in your heart for a moment now. You have seen our gratitude, deep and rich, for, Father, we came from you, we belong to you, and we return to you.

The church school teacher brings to his worship service his own understanding and experience of worship. Can he see in common places and common things the footprints of God? Can he see strawberries in the window and lift up his heart in reverence, awe, and excitement to adore God for his wonders? Can he see a lonely child in need of love and understanding and assure him of his own friendship and of God's eternal love?

If worship is to express the child's response to God's revelation, it should be as carefully planned as the worship service in the sanctuary. A teacher cannot assume that, because he worships regularly, he is an authority on worship. He needs to study in order to gain a deeper awareness of what worship is. Several good books on worship are listed in the Selected Bibliography.

Juniors and older pupils will want to know the origins and the history of worship. They need to be familiar with the worship in their own church service as well as the worship service in the temple, and in the early Christian church. They want to know the meaning of mass in the Catholic Church and how Protestant worship has evolved from it. They will be interested in the new forms of worship being tried today.

The young people want to be familiar with the meaning and the mechanics of their worship service. Three or four Sundays may be spent at the beginning of the year in helping children understand the procedure and the meaning of various steps and symbols used. A hit-and-miss worship service destroys many values the teacher aspires to cultivate in children—reverence, wonder, awe, adoration.

During the period of preparation, the teacher will extend his session on worship to the full hour and end with a short prayer. The worship service itself then becomes the climactic experience for the children toward which they have planned together thoughtfully and sensitively. Children will take turns in lighting candles, arranging the worship center, receiving the offering, reading the scripture, playing a musical instrument during the prelude or offering. It should be their worship service so that they can participate in it with a spirit of joy and celebration. A thoughtful teacher will assign responsibilities two or three weeks ahead and will inform the parents personally or through a telephone call so they can help their child in his preparation.

Mrs. Brown kept a card file for all her assignments. This assured each child of his turn. The children looked forward to participating. Children who took part in the service and the child who failed to appear on the assigned Sunday had their names moved to the back of the file. There were very few absences in that room.

A worship service should be as smooth and as orderly as the teacher can make it. But sometimes his love of order and perfection can be sacrificed for greater gains. If the child stumbles over a word, the teacher will be there to help without embarrassing him. His acceptance of the child's effort will mean a great deal. Teachers need not be afraid that the child will feel he is a performer. The child's attitude toward worship and his understanding of what worship is will minimize any such risks.

The teacher should work with his worship committee of three or four boys and girls in planning an attractive room to create the mood for worship. Flowers, meaningful worship centers, orderly chairs, the teacher's own appropriate grooming, his confident and unhurried tone of voice will effect the incentive to worship God.

The length and the content of the worship service should vary with different age-groups. It is important for the teacher to consider the child's attention span and his comprehension level —vocabulary, ability to deduce meaning from generalizations and abstractions, relevance of the central thought to his needs.

If the child has written prayers, litanies, poems, they should be incorporated into the worship service. The selection of hymns, scripture readings, prayers should emphasize the central theme that has been stressed during the instruction period. The child should go home fully aware of what the main idea was for that morning and how he·can relate what he learned to his experiences.

Worship to be meaningful should come at the end of the session and not at the beginning as "the opening exercise to quiet down the children." The word must be heard first before the child can respond to God. There is no formula for a correct order and content of the worship service. *The child learns how to worship by worshiping.*

RESOURCES FOR WORSHIP

The teacher is referred to the Bible, meaningful poetry, hymns, meditations as sources for worship aids.

Calls to worship. The Old Testament is a rich source of verses that can be used at the beginning of a worship service. Below are examples:

> O come, let us worship and bow down,
>   let us kneel before the Lord, our Maker!
> For he is our God,
>   and we are the people of his pasture,
>   and the sheep of his hand.
>   —Psalm 95:6-7

> The Lord is in his holy temple;
>   let all the earth keep silence before him.
>   —Habakkuk 2:20

Holy, holy, holy is the Lord of hosts.
—Isaiah 6:3

Come, let us go up to the mountain of the Lord,
    to the house of the God of Jacob;
that he may teach us his ways,
    and that we may walk in his paths.

.   .   .   .

Come, let us walk
    in the light of the Lord.
—Isaiah 2:3, 5

Offering responses. The Doxology is often sung as an offering response. But more than one response should be learned—the choice depending on the age level of the children. The following selections are widely used: "Father, bless the gifts we bring thee" (*Hymns for Primary Worship,* No. 169); "Thy work, O God, needs many hands" (*Hymns for Junior Worship,* No. 128); and "All things come of thee, O Lord" (*Hymns for Junior Worship,* No. 129). The hymn need not be sung every time, but can be read as a prayer. Poetry can also be used; for example, these lines from *The Vision of Sir Launfal* by James Russell Lowell:

Not what we give, but what we share,
For the gift without the giver is bare;
Who gives himself with his alms feeds three—
Himself, his hungering neighbor, and me.

Prayer responses. The *Gloria Patri* is a good prayer response. Such hymns as "Hear our prayer, O Lord" and "Let the words of my mouth" (*Hymns for Junior Worship,* Nos. 132 and 133) may also be sung.

WORSHIP CENTERS

Worship centers preach their own unique sermons. They need to create a mood of quietness and beauty symbolically or visually to call man to worship. They also need to communicate a message to emphasize and enrich the worship theme of the service. Since the worship center is the focal point of all eyes, it should be placed in full view of all children. Let the worship center tell its story. Objects referred to in the biblical story can be arranged against an interesting background. If the story is about the sower and the seed, the teacher may use seeds, weeds, and good soil. A miniature well made of clay and a pottery jar tell the story of the Samaritan woman at the well with Jesus. A bowl, sandals, towel, and water tell the feet-washing story. The teacher will want to refer to these objects in his meditation by touching them, in a manner that does not destroy the element of mystery. Let the worship center inspire the worshiper.

The teacher may not have time for all these artistic creations, but a worship committee can work with him on the projects. A creative mother who may never teach would love to be on this committee. She can help children make a triptych for a background. If the teacher plans in advance for his service, the children will be able to look for the right objects for the story. Children can make attractive designs on their altar cloths and write a verse of their choice by the simple use of spray guns and tempera paint or ink. Colored or white ironed sheets make attractive altar cloths. Art objects, sculptured works, projected slides, prints of masterpieces secured from art galleries or art books make inviting arrangements.

SPONTANEOUS WORSHIP

Who has not lifted up his heart in praise and adoration when he has seen the rain falling through the leaves, water trickling through the rocks; heard the song of the robin at daybreak; watched the sunset at twilight? Like the psalmist, man lifts up his heart in exultation and sings, "O Lord, our Lord, how majestic is thy name in all the earth!"

The teacher should be alert to all opportunities for spontaneous worship—sensing the readiness of the class, lifting the commonplace to an act of worship. There are even times when "special moments" can be brought out of bad situations.

A kindergarten teacher wrote about her experience on a Sunday morning:

> The children were looking at a bird nest which had one little real egg in it. They carefully passed the egg around the circle from one pair of cupped hands to another, exerting great care that the egg should not drop or be crushed as we talked about its being excessively fragile. Later on, Pat evidently took the egg from the nest and placed it on a chair. Bobby sat down, not noticing the egg. Bobby told me about it. I picked up the smashed, gooey egg, and took it to the wastebasket, and then I told Pat that it was too bad we no longer had the little egg for the bird nest.
>
> I was in another part of the room getting the next project set up, when Bobby again got my attention and said, "Pat is crying." Immediately I went to Pat and sat in a small chair beside him. I put my arms around him and told him that I forgave him, God forgave him, and that now he should forgive himself. And then I said, "We all make mistakes, Pat. I, too, keep doing things for which I am sorry." I dried his eyes. He blew his nose and then went ahead and drew his picture.
>
> But evidently Pat still had some feelings which had to come out. Presently, during rhythms, Kurt dissolved in tears saying, "Pat kicked me on the bottom." At this point I said, "Let's talk to God about the difficulty this time." I knelt down, putting an arm about each of the two children, and prayed. I cannot recall exactly the words I used, but it was certainly about forgiving, being kinder. You could have heard a pin drop. Every child was absolutely there. This was an authentic meeting with God. I feel quite sure every kindergartner in the room sensed his presence.
>
> When I finished and opened my eyes, instead of seeing a

Kurt with teary eyes, I saw a shining beautiful smile. Pat was smiling too.

The growth of seeds that the child planted a few weeks ago, the baby chick that came from an egg, the arrival of a new baby brother or sister into a home need to be shared. Experiences of wonder and awe set the stage for the teacher to talk about the child's "wonder part," which enables him to feel, to love, to be thankful, and to be kind to others. Many are such moments of joy when man experiences a feeling of gratitude in the common events of life and sends quiet or exalting messages to God.

MUSIC IN THE WORSHIP SERVICE

"The piano player is not here this morning," said Mrs. Lamb as she saw the superintendent passing by. "Do you know what hymns you are going to use this morning?" asked the superintendent. "Maybe I can help you." "Well," replied the teacher, "I have not thought that far ahead. They all love 'Jesus loves me'!"

If music is an essential tool for the expression of man's faith, praise, adoration, why should not some valuable time be spent learning new hymns that are recommended in denominational curriculum materials?

Some of the so-called piano players are incompetent and the teachers often do not read music or sing in tune. The trial and error, the dissonance of the music destroy the mood the teacher wants to create for his worship service. The teacher can help the situation if he makes every effort to learn the hymns in his departmental meetings and invites a competent mother to help with the music. This will give him confidence and enthusiasm when he introduces new hymns to children. If the situation does not improve, the teacher may invite an interested choir member who will record on tape the hymns that are to be learned. Autoharps and guitars are now successfully being used in church schools, and children respond enthusiastically.

It is also important to bring qualified singers to each department every three or four weeks to teach children new hymns. Twenty minutes or more should be allowed for learning the music as well as the meaning of the words. Children enjoy hymns when the words make sense to them. More theology has been learned through good music than through any other experience. Poetry and music have a way of staying with the learner and becoming a part of his thinking and feeling.

Choir directors ought to be interested in teaching hymns as well as anthems. Anthems are wonderful and deeply moving, but they should not be used exclusively. The director often steers his energies toward an accomplished performance because this is challenging to him as well as satisfying to the adult listeners in the sanctuary. Despite additional professional help in many churches, church school music suffers a poverty today which was unknown two or three decades ago. The director can add so much beauty and reverence to the worship service if he teaches hymns of adoration, hymns of dedication, and offering and prayer responses, and spends some time in explaining the theological concepts in the hymns. Children can then sing with vitality and mean what they sing.

SYMBOLS, RITES, AND RITUALS

At 7:30 every morning my friend and I visited a large, beautiful Catholic church on our way to school. We were in elementary school then and were not interested in religion per se. I still remember how reverently we knelt, crossed ourselves, smelled the burning incense, watched the devout Catholics move in and out and burn candles in front of their favorite saints. We felt surrounded by beauty and the incomprehensible mystery of life.

The music, the pageantry of this church had a strong emotional hold on us.

I am not advocating a similar experience for all children or adults, but merely stating that symbols, rites, and rituals are essential for some people's spiritual growth. Onto—and through —symbols man projects his idealism, his aspirations, his values. Man's logical mind will say that symbols in themselves do not have any power or meaning except what man ascribes to them, but all nonverbal thinking is done on the unconscious level through symbols, images, and myths over which the rational mind has very little control. Words are used by the conscious mind only in the areas where man can make verbal formulations of a concept. Man in great measure is led or guided by his unconscious mind. This is why some pageantry, ritual, symbolism, change of color in vestments, attractive altar arrangements, good music, candle-lighting can create the mood for and aid worship. They anchor man to reality because they give an objective form to ideals, and the mysteries of life become less mysterious, more understandable and workable, freeing man from his feelings of despair and helplessness.

Protestant churches today make extensive use of symbols. They are seen on the altar, in the vestments of the clergy, in the designs of altar cloths, in the architecture of buildings, in stained-glass windows, in paintings, murals, sculptured objects. The religious symbols used today have been handed down by early Christians. The events in Jesus' life had such great emotional impact on his disciples that they referred to him as the Good Shepherd, the Lamb of God, and so on. Whenever they wanted to remember a particular event, they referred to a symbol to signify it. Children can learn to appreciate symbols because symbols refer to the roots of their past and link them to the idealism of their fathers.

Symbols appear in various forms—words, names, objects, signs, figures, colors, and monograms. The meaning of symbols can be explained to the pupil by going back to the events in church history. The explanation should be given in a manner that is understandable for the learner at his age. There are a number of great ideas in the Christian faith that cannot be totally understood by the child, but through appropriate symbols he can begin to grasp the ideas for which they stand. Meaning can unfold with the child's increasing maturity. Symbols tell their story and are remembered because they satisfy an emotional need. The cross is such a symbol.

Other commonly used symbols are IHS or IHC—the first letters of the Greek word IHCOYC meaning Jesus; X and P—Chi Rho—from the Greek *Christos,* meaning "the anointed." The church is often represented by an ark or a ship.

SYMBOLIC MOVEMENT

There is an increasing appreciation of the art of symbolic movement in many churches as a medium of expression of innermost feelings. It is known by various names—interpretive movement, modern or sacred dance, creative movement. The leader carefully chooses a hymn, a poem, a psalm, or music that best lends itself to interpretation of meaning and feeling through graceful body movements. He helps the participants in their efforts to express their emotions—sorrow, despair, praise, gratitude, joy—but they do their own feeling and thinking. Persons have to enter into the experience wholeheartedly really to know renewal and healing.

For effective involvement teachers need to become acquainted with the books of Margaret Fisk Taylor—*Time for Wonder, Time for Discovery, Look Up and Live, Symbolic Dance and Worship* (United Church Press, 1967). The author explains the procedures for interpreting hymns and stories through movements.

Symbolic movement is used in Christmas pageants, in Easter

sunrise services, in Palm Sunday parades, in rallies, in outdoor and indoor vesper services, in the morning worship service both in the sanctuary and in the church school.

Creative expression in all its forms affirms man's dignity. Through it man develops an "intuitive familiarity," a new perspective to view life with a sense of wonder and surprise, and finds himself at home in his universe.

Symbols, music, creative movement, silence, beauty call man to worship God. Each man responds in his own way and in his own time. The teacher will communicate to his pupil his own obligation and need to worship God in awe and reverence. The pupil, thus encouraged, will strive to penetrate into the depths of his own life, and of God, and of God's universe. Together teacher and pupil will discover all around them what Paul Tillich has called the "joy that has eternity within it."

Chapter Seven

Parents, Key Teachers of Religion

I have chosen him, that he may charge his children and his household after him to keep the way of the Lord by doing righteousness and justice.
—GENESIS 18:19

THE FAMILY HERITAGE

The letter for which everyone was anxiously waiting arrived. Albert had gone abroad for graduate study, and soon the war broke out. He wrote:

Dear Father,

Days are dark as nights here. I have been very close to death several times. Bombs exploded all around me. I heard the cries of the dying. I saw men, women, and children burn in the streets. I live in a nightmare. I am writing to let you know how grateful I am for the faith you have given me. Even in my darkest hour when I feel I am in the valley of death I feel God's presence with me.

Your son,
Albert

His father read the letter several times. Tears were rolling down his cheeks—tears of sorrow for his son's distress and agony, and tears of joy that he was not walking alone.

Marvin Himmel, presently a producer of entertainment programs, remembers his father's concern before he allowed his thirteen-year-old son to join a tour:

> You come from a good home, your family heritage is proud, you have been taught the understanding of your religious faith. As you travel through life observe all, and that which is right live with; and that which is wrong, even in some small way try to improve. If a man walks in darkness, he walks the longest and coldest road . . . alone.[1]

What greater legacy can parents leave their children! So many provide only a feeding station during the day and a parking lot at night. But a child cannot live by bread alone; life makes many intricate demands for which he needs resources of strength. He turns to his parents for a firm foundation of faith on which to build his moral, ethical, and spiritual life. This is certainly a right and realistic expectation. But some parents are timid and afraid to assume this responsibility because they are not sure of their own personal faith, while others are so preoccupied with establishing themselves professionally and socially that they postpone this obligation to a future date—until it is too late. In some homes there is a definite division of responsibility: the father is the breadwinner; the mother reluctantly and exhaustedly assumes her role as teacher, disciplinarian, guide, and friend of their children.

Parents are the key teachers of religion. Whether they make a conscious effort to transmit their faith or show lethargy, they influence the child for good or ill. How the child thinks of God and how he relates to other people is most often a reflection of

---

[1] Marvin Himmel, "This I Believe," *Chicago Daily News*, October 17, 1960, p. 42.

the thinking and feeling of his parents. If he experiences love in his home as the supreme power for good, he expresses love in his relationships; if his parents feel force is the essential ingredient of life, the child will often be involved in fist fights under the guise of self-defense. If he is prevented from playing with others in the neighborhood because of differences in race, culture, or socioeconomic level, he may grow to feel that "you only play with your own kind." Children mirror their parents especially in early childhood when they are more impressionable and spend more time at home. This period is crucial because what the parents sow then, the child will reap later.

If children are the most precious gifts God has entrusted to parents, should not their overriding concern be to permeate their home with the Christian faith that results in Christian living?

Walter Schirra, Sr., the father of one of America's astronauts, shared with a reporter his understanding of his responsibility:

> There's a lot of me in Wally, and there ought to be a lot of every father in every son. . . .
>
> A son needs someone to talk with, and too many sons find they can't confide in their fathers. . . . A father has to have time to talk with his son. . . . A father has to inspire his son, because boys can so often be distracted from important things.
>
> A father is a teacher. He shows his son and he tells his son, but the boy has to do it himself. . . .
>
> A father should love his son—in a manly way. And he should let his son know about his love, that it's real and deep and lasting, that he'll stand by his son and be there if ever he should call.[2]

Many forces in our culture are pressuring parents to split their loyalties and move in different and often opposite directions; of course this causes a great deal of instability in the home. The church faces a great challenge and much responsibility, for the

---

[2] Walter M. Schirra, Sr., as told to Mark Howat, "How to Raise a Hero," *This Week* magazine, February 3, 1963, pp. 5 f.

responsibility for the development of Christian family life falls on its Christian education forces. The church must guide, nurture, and inspire parents who need its help.

CHURCH CONCERN FOR THE FAMILY

"He that would teach would learn," said Chaucer. Parents want to be well grounded in the Christian faith in order to have adequate inner resources for tough times as well as for everyday living. This is every man's lifelong quest for meaning, for fulfillment. The church opens wide its doors to help parents in their search. Such resources cannot be provided in an instant-kit. They come in small packages. The word must be heard regularly so that ideas register in the mind and provide food for thought. The growth of man depends on his decision to say "yes" to God's claim on him. "They have not all heeded the gospel; for Isaiah says, 'Lord, who has believed what he has heard from us?' So faith comes from what is heard, and what is heard comes by the preaching of Christ" (Rom. 10:16-17).

A man recently commented, "The church has let us down. It does not provide the inspiration it used to. It does not motivate us to become better Christians." This gentleman was once an active member of the church. He now expected all inspiration to come to him from the sermon on Sunday morning. He was standing on the fringe of the church and reaping the marginal benefits. It is wise to remember the words of Jesus, "Whoever seeks to gain his life will lose it, but whoever loses his life will preserve it" (Luke 17:33).

Since religion is taught in every home, consciously or unconsciously, it is the responsibility of the church to guide parents in making this education Christian. The minister invites members and friends of his church to participate in the activities of the church—the Sunday morning worship service, the education program in all its phases, the stewardship and mission outreach, counseling, music, fellowship organizations, home calls. Active participation brings transformation. If a man invests his whole self in some worthwhile endeavor, if he opens himself to be aware of his inner and outer world, then he becomes free to respond to life. But freedom is an achievement; it is man's independence nurtured by man's faith and dependence on God.

The minister seeks the counsel and the active support of his committee or board of Christian education to provide for parents the quality of education that will best cultivate this dependence on God. Guidance is given through short-term parent institutes, grade meetings to acquaint parents with the children's study, devotional material for family worship, a library of helpful books, family festivals, seasonal workshops, adult education.

Open house for parents. Some teachers have opened their homes for an intimate discussion of what goes on in the child's classroom on Sunday morning. They have discussed content, methods, resource materials, music. Many parents have been touched by such hospitality, warmth, and enthusiasm. Some teachers invite parents to a Sunday morning session. In one instance each child wrote an invitation to his parents, who also received in the mail a letter and a bulletin showing their child's particular responsibility at the open house.

The junior department held an evening open house. The parents were divided into three buzz groups to discuss the question "Is it right for the father to take a fishing trip on Sunday morning and expect his son to attend church school?" As the parents labored with the problem and expressed their pros and cons they became aware of new insights into their unique responsibility as Christian teachers.

The lower junior department held a typical departmental meeting to which parents were invited. They planned for the next four sessions, thinking through their objectives, content, methods to be used, resources, worship. They reviewed filmstrips and chose the one they liked best. Then each teacher volunteered for a particular responsibility for a month. At the end of their session, when the superintendent invited the parents to comment, they said, "It is unbelievable that so much thought and planning go into each session. We are delighted with your work and grateful to each and every one of you."

For two months orientation sessions were held for parents in the evenings and on Sunday afternoons. Each family received a carefully planned mimeographed booklet with pages of assorted colors which outlined the curriculum for the whole year, hymns the child would learn, information about the library, dates to remember, and suggestions to parents as to how they might work with teachers.

Each department assumed some responsibility in preparing the booklet. It was hard work, but it paid dividends. One teacher remarked, "I read so many books on the subject, spent so many hours thinking through my own philosophy and techniques, I honestly feel that teaching is a very rewarding experience for me as a parent, for better understanding of my own children and their needs."

Every year the teachers varied the nature and content of their open house. They stayed away from stereotyped patterns. If a teacher is failing to reach the parents it may be wise for him to review and evaluate the approach.

Family festivals. When families move to a new community they often look to the church for help. They want to get acquainted with other families and find new friends for their children. This can be accomplished in the church through monthly or seasonal festivals, which are planned to provide fun, fellowship, opportunities for creative thinking, and the experience of worship.

During a creative-thinking period the parents may sit in a circle and consider such topics as family worship, the worship center, the use of the Bible in the home, the study of religion through the eyes of contemporary artists, the significance of the family council, the family's mission outreach, right or wrong in day-to-day family living.

Each church should devise its own pattern of festival. There should be enough variety to create excitement. It is important to remember that children should not be sent to another room for comic-strip entertainment while parents are listening to a lecture. Children may not absorb all the content, but neither do all the parents. Children catch the mood and absorb the psychological atmosphere so important for family relationships. In today's culture there are many forces pulling people apart; the family festival is one specific activity that unites the family. Children see their parents in a new light as people capable of having fun with them and with other families. After a family festival, a young woman related her experience:

> I left home at an early age because of the many tensions between my mother and myself. Recently Mother came to visit me and I brought her to our family festival. When she saw my love for the church and the people, she felt she had lost something important in her living. My mother is a professional woman. She was too preoccupied with her work and she failed to give the love and attention that I needed so desperately when I was growing up. After the evening was over, we went home and sat quietly and looked at each other. To my surprise she said, "I guess this is what we missed in our relationship. We had no common experience to talk about, no meeting of minds, no warmth in our relationship. I am happy for you and your family."

Stewardship and mission. Parents encourage and discuss the annual service projects for the church school—UNICEF, Thanksgiving, Christmas, and Lent offerings in money, food, clothing, medicine, and so on. The superintendent or treasurer of the church explains to parents how children are given choices as to what to give and where to send it and for what purpose. One year children preferred to give milk rather than provide scholarship money. For several years they provided medicine for people in India through their medical missionary. All such projects can be promoted through letters sent to the homes, articles in the church and local newspapers, information to children through posters, slides, speakers, and trips. Parents learn where the money goes and how it is used. They can help their children to understand too.

When one little girl came home with her money in her pocket, her mother asked why she had not put it into the offering plate. The child remarked, "Jesus has more money than I do."

But another child, discovering the desperate need of children in India for food and medicine, gave all the money he had received on his birthday. When his mother asked if he would not consider saving some of it for his own use, he replied, "Mother, I have everything; they have nothing."

Adult education. Classes in adult education try to provide the spiritual resources necessary for personal growth. The strength of the classes does not lie in the wealth of information the leader has, important as this is, but in the dialogue among members: Celia evaluates her thinking in the light of what Jim said; no one actually attempts to arrive at a consensus. As they probe together the inner-world-space of the mind, which can be understood only through introspection and soul-searching, they come to understand their own Christian faith, themselves, their children, and their fellowmen. After many sessions in study and thought, a young adult remarked, "I have never been able to talk as freely as this before. I have shed a burden that was weighing heavily on my heart. I am grateful not only to the leader but to all the members for freeing me from my bondage." An attractive woman, after a profound experience, looked at each individual in the room and said, "I love everyone in this group." Lasting and meaningful friendships develop when a person shares his self intimately and genuinely and is loved and accepted with his limitations.

The methods used in these groups must suit the objectives. If lecture is the chosen method, then the group is interested primarily in content. Workshops improve skills. Problem-solving, role-playing, debates, panel discussions, symposia, and forums will stimulate thought and clarify ideas. Every one of these methods should conclude with a discussion so the group can experience a dynamic interaction.

The call to serve. Every layman—every mother and father as well as every unmarried adult—is a minister of his church and the church universal, and he should assume his responsibility according to his interest and ability. Growth takes place through replenishment and output. A man who expects only to receive is like stagnant water. The church urgently needs qualified people with dedication and willingness to learn and to teach. Married couples are needed to serve as teams in all departments beginning with the nursery. It is not *convenient* for any man or woman to teach, but the challenge is to the brave. It is a challenge to those who believe in the infinite worth of every child as a child of God, and endeavor to awaken the child to this realization. Grenfell found joy when he chose for himself the hazardous road and out of his experience was born the conclusion that real joy comes not from ease of riches, or even from the praise of men, but from doing something worthwhile.

FAMILY WORSHIP IN THE SANCTUARY

"We believe in the values the church stands for and tries to cultivate in our children," said a mother. "In our family everyone is expected to attend church and church school. It is absurd to ask a child, 'Do you want to take a bath?' He just takes a

bath. We say, 'Now we shall ————.' It is as simple as that."
Interested parents can interest their uninterested children. Worshiping together as a family is an experience all children enjoy.
Little children love the "big church." Worshiping as a family
gives them a sense of security and a feeling that their church is
not a building but a community of faith. A children's story in
the service and a familiar hymn will help the young worshiper to
feel at home.

Where two Sunday services are held, parents should be encouraged to worship as a family one session and attend church
school and adult education the next session. Children in their
formative and impressionable years should be exposed to the
music, the pageantry, the symbols, and the beauty around them.
And adults should learn to appreciate their presence at the
Sunday service.

It is often argued that the disadvantages of this arrangement
outweigh its advantages. But the two-session plan makes it possible for teachers to receive the necessary inspiration and be well
grounded in their own Christian faith through church attendance. It also enables husbands and wives to teach who would
not do so if teaching were to prevent their worshiping together.

If the two-session plan is not feasible, arrangements should at
least be made so children may, at regular intervals, attend church
with their parents instead of attending church school.

Albert Schweitzer, speaking of his own experience, said:

> From the services in which I joined as a child I have taken
> with me into life a feeling for what is solemn, and a need for
> quiet and self-recollection, without which I cannot realize the
> meaning of my life. I cannot, therefore, support the opinion of
> those who would not let children take part in grown-up peo-
> ple's services till they to some extent understand them. The
> important thing is not that they shall understand, but that they
> shall feel something of what is serious and solemn. The fact
> that the child sees his elders full of devotion, and has to feel

something of their devotion himself, that is what gives the service its meaning for him.[3]

Each generation knowingly and deliberately should transmit to the next generation the values that stem from religion. To bring meaning into a meaningless society, to bring love into a world filled with hatred needs the support and cooperation of all the forces acting upon society. Christian parents and the concerned church ought certainly to be aware of the urgency of their mission.

---

[3] Albert Schweitzer, *Memoirs of Childhood and Youth* (New York: Macmillan, 1931), p. 62.

Chapter Eight

Discipline

*He who is slow to anger is better
than the mighty,
and he who rules his spirit than
he who takes a city.*
—PROVERBS 16:32

A LONG-RANGE PLAN

"You sound just like my principal," he said angrily. "I have heard all that jazz before." Bob was in my office because he had been disturbing his class. His teacher's many efforts to reach him had failed. My effort to make him aware of my confidence in him as a young man with a great potential for good was unsuccessful also.

Bob was an intelligent junior high pupil but loud and crude. He argued and debated and tried to outsmart his peers and his teacher. There were many tense moments in the classroom, and the patience of his teacher sometimes reached the breaking point. But Bob had a soft streak in him that made him lovable. His face glowed when ideas stirred his imagination and led him to think beyond what was being taught. Following a talk by his super-intendent at a worship service, he walked to her and asked sev-eral searching questions. It became obvious that Bob deeply re-sented the second marriage of his mother. He liked the man and tolerated him as a father, but he felt guilty about his feelings and showed this strain in various forms of rebellion. The super-intendent put her hand on his shoulder and let him know that she really cared how he felt. "Bob," she said, "I know several young people who have not had even one good father, and you have had two." As the conversation progressed, Bob realized that he had never viewed the problem this way before. "Thank you," he said and walked away with bowed head, immersed in thought.

In the fall Bob did not return to the church school. I saw his mother one day, and inquired about him. "Tell him," I said, "that I missed him."

The following Sunday, Bob made an effort to pass by my office. I went out to greet him and said with outstretched hand, "Bob, it's so good to see you!"

"Thank you," he said, and walked to his classroom.

In the next four years Bob found a home in the church. People cared how he felt. His inquisitive mind sought answers to the ultimate questions of life. The classroom discussions nurtured both his mind and his spirit. He showed phenomenal growth. At one session, he presented an excellent paper on the relation-ship between science and religion. It showed wide research. Bob is now stretching his mind in a highly reputable college.

We teachers are often tempted to look at situations like Bob's as emergency problems calling for immediate control, usually in the form of punishment. Bob was disturbing because he was dis-turbed. He was desperately looking for help. If Jimmy is de-structive, Billy is hurting other children, Sue is showing off, they are simply saying, "Look, I have an urgent problem. Do some-thing about it!" Immediate controls are necessary in emergency situations, but it would be wrong to assume that they will bring a lasting change in the behavior of the child.

We need to think of discipline as a long-range plan of training to help the child to develop an inner control or inner compass so that he himself is able to determine the direction of his behavior, what to sanction and what to condone. This depends on his increasing maturity which develops through the years as he takes the initiative to evaluate his own reactions to threatening and novel situations.

No problem in human relationships can be compartmentalized and made the sole domain of any one particular group—the home, the school, or organizations. They all have a mutual concern and a common goal: to effect the optimum desirable change in the self to enable the child to bring about harmony and balance between the restrictions of the outer world and his urge to express his inner drives. Discipline, therefore, is not an administrative method, meting out penalties for offenses. It is a program of guidance engendering desirable attitudes.

What the child needs is a noble self-image which will determine his mental health and future success and happiness. Fostering mental health in each child is just as important as developing skills and storing knowledge—if not more so—though the latter are often necessary to achieve the former.

Inexperienced teachers, in particular, try to be so loving and kind that sometimes they fail to take direct action, especially at the beginning of the year when it is so crucial. They mistakenly feel that in a church such firmness is cause for guilt. On the contrary, the previous discussion does not preclude the necessity, indeed, the desirability occasionally, of resorting to such measures as separation from the group; withdrawal of privilege; talks with parents; removal from classroom, perhaps accompanied by a high school helper. Such measures are, however, negative—no problem is solved; and they should be followed as soon as possible by an encounter between teacher and pupil where there is an effort to rebuild the relationship and rescue the youngster's ego or self-image.

There are a number of ways by which self-discipline can be nurtured in the church school and in the home.

THE ROLE OF THE TEACHER

The teacher's view of himself. The church school teacher needs to indulge in some honest self-exploration. This is difficult but very significant. He brings to his important task a certain emotional load—his likes and dislikes, concern over some physical illness in his own family, fatigue, insufficient sleep, or a disturbing breakfast on Sunday morning. Any one of these may well make him irritable in situations that perhaps should not call for negative reaction.

The teacher may identify the misdemeanor of a child with his own lack of experience in teaching. He shows despair in his face and tone: "I am not cut out to be a teacher." "I do not know how to cope with all these problems." "The kids are smarter than I am. I do not know how to answer their questions." To disguise his feelings of fear and frustration, he gives militant orders and acts like an authoritarian teacher who has figured out all the dos and don'ts. He is impulsive, and sometimes without meaning to be so he is rude.

The self-confident teacher shows a different picture. He has authority; he has know-how. He is relaxed and moves easily from one child to another, from one activity to another, without fuss or rush. He thinks of himself as a maturing person and brings to his task flexibility, warmth, acceptance, and love. He talks less and listens more. He keeps his eyes open and watches what is happening within the group. His security helps him to absorb a reasonable amount of hostility. He delegates responsibility as well as authority with no fear of the consequences. He allows the child to make mistakes and learn from his errors. He is available for help if the child calls for it. This approach makes the child feel that his teacher believes in him and in his ability to be productive. The student in turn calls to action all his creative energies to be worthy of the teacher's expectations as well as to satisfy his own need for self-fulfillment.

The teacher's view of the child. Growing up is a painful process. The child does not understand all the changes that are taking place within him—physical, emotional, and intellectual. He experiences confusion, fear, frustration. There are conflicts and stresses in his own home. His parents pressure him to excel academically and socially to satisfy their own search for status in their community. There is sibling rivalry, and there are broken homes where one parent assumes the role of both and all too often adds misery and confusion to the child's life. Alcoholism, adoption, overprotection or indifference, mental illness, mobility from one state to another—any one of these problems may uproot a child. He is lonely in a crowd where, he feels, no one cares what happens to him. These are the children who come for help. They are neither angels nor devils, but they have the potential to become either.

Teachers usually have fewer problems with girls. Studies show that girls are more intuitive and figure out the teacher and give him what he wants. Boys are more objective, precise, analytical, and demanding. The teacher must deserve their loyalty and support. If he does that, he is the hero they admire and follow.

A child may indicate his stress by trying to attract attention—clowning, excessive boasting, loudness, clumsiness, lying, cheating, tattling. He may try to assert his powers by being destructive, bullying, resorting to temper tantrums, fighting, or showing anger. He may display his inefficiency and seek exemptions from required performance by stuttering, blushing, being a loner, or acting frightened. All these add up to what the child thinks about himself—his feeling of worthlessness and inadequacy. The sensitive teacher will accept and understand all these strains. He will talk with the student privately and show him that there are more acceptable forms of behavior. "Maybe you had a tough day today; we all do sometimes. I understand how you feel. . . ." "I like you, Sam, you are a fine boy; but I don't like the way you hurt Leon. Whenever you feel like hurting someone, take this punching bag and hit it as hard as you want, or pound this clay until you feel better." Children are action-oriented; they do not need lectures to which they turn deaf ears. Rather, their negative impulses need to be channeled into more constructive outlets. Once the hostilities are released, a child will be ready to move in with the group as a desirable member.

The basic philosophy of the teacher. A sound philosophy of Christian education is a teacher's road map. This will determine his goal, his direction, and more or less the outcome. It will clarify reasons for teaching—its meaning and the significance of commitment. This philosophy cannot be handed down. It comes from study, research, evaluation of concepts in the light of present-day theology. It must be a discovery which through use will be internalized and become consciously and unconsciously a part of the teacher's thinking and acting. This means finding answers to the fundamental questions underlying growth in all its dimensions: What is the teacher's concept of the child—all good, all bad? What are some of the techniques he could use, and why? Are they ends in themselves or means to an end? What are some of the theological concepts he has to deal with? Are they personal convictions or borrowed ideas?

The teacher's knowledge of his subject matter. Exciting and inspiring teachers can breathe life into dull materials that may be boring to children. No curriculum is perfect. The teacher can add his own personal resources and make children feel that together they are probing the important questions in life. His zeal, enthusiasm, and versatility will make them want to rise above their personal pettiness because he commands their respect. Paul sat at the feet of Gamaliel, Plato at the feet of Socrates, Peter at the feet of Jesus. They drank deeply from the fountain of knowledge and insight, transforming not only themselves but later generations. Inspiring teachers are free from conformity. They study at the feet of masters, but they think for themselves and help their own pupils to catch a glimpse of their enthusiasm. Such learning is volitional, not superimposed. It will not inspire resentment, rebellion, and fear of being manipulated.

The psychological climate. The teacher's warmth as he greets children at the door, his careful planning of the lesson in all its details so it will meet the needs of individual children, an attractive room planned and arranged by children can give the kind of beauty that is loved and accepted by children. This is not the description of a utopia or the vision of a dreamer. It is simply the elimination of all the hurdles, the clutter, which may induce an adverse reaction.

On Sunday morning and during the week, every sensitive teacher prays for strength for tough times, for wisdom to find the right answers to trying situations.

Help me to see today's missteps in perspective against the long road he must go, and grant me the grace of patience with his slow pace.

Give me the precious wisdom of knowing when to smile at the small mischiefs of age and when to give him the haven of firmness against the impulses, which in his heart he fears and cannot master.

In time of needed punishment, give me a warm heart and a gentle voice so he may feel the rule of order in his friend and clasp it to his soul to be his conscience.

Help me to hear the anguish in his heart through the din of angry words or across the gulf of brooding silence; and having heard, give me the grace to bridge the gap between us with understanding warmth before speaking my own quick retorts, and stay my tongue also from the words that chill his confiding in me.

Still from my voice and smooth from my brow all that mars infectious serenity and joy in living; rather let my face so shine that these later years will seem to him a promised land toward which to strive.

I pray that I may raise my voice more in joy at what he is than in vexation at what he has done; so each day he may grow in sureness of himself.

Help me to hold him with such warmth as will give him friendliness toward his fellowman; then give me the fortitude to free him to go strongly on his way.

When I see him striding forward eagerly, self-sure, friendly, and in good conscience, my grateful heart will swell with joy.[1]

THE ROLE OF THE HOME

"Why do you talk about study, assignments, regular attendance?" asked a parent. "Children are pressured in every community. Let them have fun at the church school." If by fun the parent means entertainment as an escape from the anxieties of life, certainly the church school does not view its responsibility in this light. Such fun kills time; in the church school we teachers use time. Such fun interferes with serious living and thinking. We make an honest effort to provide the opportunities where the child learns to face reality and cope with it. This is the place where he feels free to ask questions about the ultimate meaning of life and finds some answers.

Some parents are called "the dumpers" because they think of the church school as a glorified baby-sitting bureau. Occasionally children are asked to attend two sessions, allowing enough time

---

[1] "A Teacher's Prayer" by James Parker, Director of the Covina, California, Human Relations Center. Used by permission.

for parents to play golf leisurely or attend to household chores. If the church is not important to the parents, the child can hardly be expected to be interested in church school.

Studies point out that there is a low correlation between intelligence and ethical behavior. The child may be familiar with all the acceptable mores and values of society, but he is also a person with his own will power. He may refuse to comply with mores and values that are not nurtured and practiced in his home. In his home he will learn to respect the necessary limits and a certain amount of freedom to enable him to declare his own independence in areas which do not interfere with the well-being of the rest of the family. These experiences are then carried to other areas of life outside the home.

Children should know what is expected of them. Some parents remind the child hastily on Sunday morning, "Now be sure you behave in Sunday school." This is a lecture delivered many times. Actually the child never hears it. To a casual question of a parent, "What did you learn in Sunday school?" the child returns a glib answer, "The same as last Sunday." A parent's attitude toward the teacher, his verbal or written expression of appreciation, his interest in the curriculum, his attendance at various functions where his awareness can be sharpened, goes a long way in making church school important for the child. Children need reasons for the things they do, just as adults do.

There is a universal lament today that there is a decline of respect for parental authority and law. Children take the upper hand and dictate the policies at home. Parents are afraid to antagonize their children. They rationalize their behavior and shield them for fear of losing face in the community. Parents of a teenager who was caught in a theft pleaded, "Please do not tell anyone. We can't live in this community if this ever becomes public knowledge."

Teachers can rejoice that the pendulum is now swinging back and that parents are increasingly assuming more authority, feeling responsible for the consequences of their child's behavior. Psychiatrist Francis Bower, in an address to the State Council of City and Village School Superintendents in Kiamesha Lake, New York, said:

> Put aside the ridiculous notion that we should be pals to our children and return to being their parents. How can discipline be obtained between father and son if the former abdicates his position to become "old-buddy-boy"? What respect can parents expect if, in order to be pals, they divest themselves of all dignity and join the adolescents they should be leading?[2]

Prof. Gilbert Highet says: "You can give a child as much love as it can absorb and still make him an idiot unfit to face the world; while the best and surest way to control our children is to explain the rules you intend to enforce."[3]

No family is exempt from problems, and they appear in varying degrees of intensity. Faulty communication seems to be always at its root. The teacher is aware of the value of the family council as a clearinghouse for ideas in his home and will recommend it to parents in their homes. Discussion may be in the areas of budget, the family car, allowances, television, dating, bedtime, the right and wrong of an action of a member. There is always a certain amount of creative tension in all these discussions because of the diversity of interests.

Children do not need more material goods but more understanding of the values the family cherishes and upholds. The child will learn at home that some situations call for restrictions and controls and others for freedom and responsibility to make choices and account for the outcome. Through such relationships the child becomes aware of his parents' faith in him. He feels

---

[2] Quoted in *Today's Child*, November, 1962, p. 7. Copyright, Today's Child Newsmagazine, 1225 Broadway, New York 10001.

[3] Gilbert Highet, *The Art of Teaching* (Vintage Books; New York: Random House, 1955), p. 235.

his ideas are respected even though challenged at times. In the absence of such assurance the child will harbor doubts about his own self-worth. He will not engage in any activity where there is the risk of failing. His feeling of acceptance and rejection is very much fostered or hindered by the emotional atmosphere in his home.

Alan, the son of two professional parents, suffered from parental indifference. Despite his high IQ, his performance was mediocre. Mrs. Bacon, his teacher, fully aware of his needs, created many opportunities to coach the boy personally. Alan showed marked improvement, and the teacher hoped that the parents would notice the change. But they did not. "Your parents are very busy people," said Mrs. Bacon, "I am sure they are interested in you and love you." "No," Alan said in tears, "they don't care what happens to me. If they are too busy for me, then I don't want them as my parents."

Family morale is the key to the presence or absence of feelings of security in the child. These feelings will manifest themselves in other experiences of his life.

STEPS IN GUIDANCE

These procedures have worked for me in the area of discipline:

1. Make sure you have a problem. Often the normal behavior of a child is interpreted as mischief. Determine what is a natural developmental characteristic or need at his stage of growth.

2. Study the child in his own setting. Locate causes for strained relationships at home, in school, with you as a teacher, or with his peers. Make sure that the diagnosis you have made as to the cause of his misbehavior is the underlying cause and not what appears to be the obvious cause. Children have a tendency to conceal the real cause to protect themselves and resent

it if they are misunderstood. Find out if a child has a physical handicap and how he feels about it. Analyze the why and the when of his behavior. Ask yourself, "What satisfaction does he get from this behavior, and how does this relate to the kind of person he wants to become?" A dialogue between the pupil and teacher in privacy is necessary for this discovery. *The ear is the road to the heart.*

3. Establish a sound relationship:

a. Recognize the pupil as a person in his own right, but do not forget he is a child and not an adult.

b. Make him feel that you are for him and not against him. Even the most impulsive ones, once they are sure you are on their side, will comply and want to be helped.

c. Inspire faith in him regarding his ability to do what he wants to do—perhaps with a little help from you.

d. Approve ten times to every one time of disapproval. Avoid at all times ridicule and sarcasm, which may destroy his sense of worth.

e. Reward a genuine improvement that has meaning for him. Remember that even a sincere glance to acknowledge a good action can be very rewarding.

f. Give him the necessary amount of responsibility in areas where he is capable of carrying things out himself. Let him use his own yardstick of excellence. Motivate him to take pride in his own accomplishment. Help him to raise his sights where he can.

g. Plan for out-of-class activities—beach parties, picnics, trips, hikes, holiday parties. Let the children know you as a friend who cares and loves.

4. Make clear the rules for expected behavior. Let your instructions be simple and specific, and repeat them often. Common rules can be worked out by the children at the beginning of the year, but they should be subject to change when the need arises.

Encourage the children to request review of unnecessary or out-grown rules.

5. Consistency and persistency in your demands and expectations make the child respect you as a teacher.

6. Ignore *trivial* misbehavior. If it continues, introduce humor or temporary isolation without later reference to the incident.

7. Stand close or seat yourself next to the child who has the tendency to disturb.

8. When a situation calls for scolding, walk to the child and tell him how you feel. Be firm but not mean. Be honest about your feelings; children detect and detest pretense.

9. When you feel the urge to lecture, give it in small doses.

10. Predict or foresee problems and eliminate stumbling blocks.

a. Take care of your needs for supplies ahead of time. Do not leave your room without adult supervision provided.

b. Display your schedule, for children need the security of a certain amount of routine.

c. Do not give choices if you have one project in mind. Do not ask, "Would you like to work with clay?" Rather, say, "We shall now work with clay." If you ask a question, you must be ready to accept a "no."

d. Do not rush children from one activity to another. It is not easy for them to shift gears.

e. Children resent orders. Issue orders only in emergency situations in a tone that demands immediate obedience and explain later if necessary.

f. Start your class with the arrival of the first child. Plan to use his help in last-minute preparation. You have set the mood for order.

g. Be in the classroom before the first child. *This is very important.*

11. Have a sense of humor. Do not take yourself too seriously. Learn how to laugh at yourself or laugh with a child.

12. In dealing with a particular problem, ask the child to make promises to himself, not to you. Ask him what he will do to keep his promises. Get across to him that you believe he believes in fair play and speak in a tone that makes him believe you have faith in your own words.

13. When you are inclined to say "Don't" be sure you have an alternative arrangement for a "do."

14. Use common sense at all times. This means, call forth your instinct which usually leads you to love and understanding. It may call you to punishment. Use your best judgment. No two children are alike; they all need different treatment. Act as a clearheaded person having your emotions well under control.

15. Talk a problem over with the parents in private, preferably during a home call. Remember the child is sacred to his parents, but they do not want you to shield their child. They want to know how they can work with you as a team. Be sensitive to their feelings; and no matter what the reaction is, you have done your share. You have given them something to think about and a basis from which to start.

16. How you say what you say is terribly important. A pleasant voice, a mobile face, graceful gestures to bring to life your ideas will captivate an audience.

17. Like your children. Enjoy being with them and working with them. Some teachers love their pupils but do not like them. Children sense the difference. The teacher who likes them, they trust all the way.

Chapter Nine

The Fellowship of Seekers

Jesus said, . . . "I am the way, and the truth, and the life; no one comes to the Father, but by me. If you have known me, you would have known my Father also; henceforth you know him and have seen him."

—JOHN 14:6-7

THE QUEST FOR CERTAINTY

"Is it true that when we go to college we dump our religion into the wastebasket?" asked Lynn at the senior-year orientation session. The room was suddenly hushed, and all eyes were fixed on me. These young people hoped that I could give them an answer that would enable them to preserve the values that had sacredness and meaning for them. They dreaded the possibility of an inner void at the center of their lives. They were afraid that when their faith was tested they would not have the courage and the fortitude to hold to the significant. They talked about boys, clothes, dormitory facilities, budget nonchalantly; but the questions of faith, meaning, and religion were their ultimate concern.

Every thinking person many times in his life questions the

real ground of truth. He finds himself incapable of coping with the seeming meaninglessness within his own life and all the life surrounding him. In his despair he longs for the fullness of the Spirit, as one longs for a fresh breath of air to relieve suffocation.

But how does he fill this void with meaning? What is meaning? What is the truth for which he is to search with all his soul?

Church school teachers who are sensitive to the significance of their responsibility to prepare a child for a Christian life often find themselves inadequate. It is not easy for them to communicate their own faith to another person. A boy expressed this predicament: "I kind of feel God and I think I know him, but I cannot explain him to you." This is true for most of us teachers because our faith is our own meeting with God, a dynamic relationship, a discovery of our own self and God, which cannot be defined or limited through dogmas, creeds, rites, and rituals.

Man will never cease trying to explain God, because important discoveries have to be shared to attain meaning and significance. Every age has its own brand of theology. Each school of thought has its own exponents and devoted followers who claim their exclusive rights to the absolute truth. Why do men—so alike in essential things—think so differently in matters of faith?

It would be much simpler if an authoritative person could tell us teachers what we should believe. We certainly would have confidence in his honesty, integrity, knowledge, and insight. But after he has told us all about his faith, he has told us about *his* faith. Our minds rebel against being told and we demand the freedom to think for ourselves in ascertaining the principles underlying the faith we hope to accept as the ground for truth. Only the person with the herd mind accepts the given and follows without resistance.

"By what authority are you doing these things?" asked the chief priests. Jesus did not give a pat answer; he countered with a question. Each priest was urged to examine his faith and look into the meaning of the alternative answers. Man's mind cannot function in a vacuum. Thought, reflection, and intuition have their origin in knowledge. The mind has to be nourished so that ideas may be looked at critically and their authenticity verified in life experiences.

The three fountains of knowledge in matters of faith that have commanded the respect of the mind and the heart are the Bible, the church, and Jesus Christ. All these must ultimately be interpreted in terms of man's own experience.

THE BIBLE AS AUTHORITY

Paul wrote to Timothy: "From childhood you have been acquainted with the sacred writings which are able to instruct you for salvation through faith in Jesus Christ" (2 Tim. 3:15). Paul refers to sources of information—the sacred writings—which relate the teachings, experiences, and insights of unique men and Jesus Christ; Paul's reference is made to historical facts and not to the interpretations of these facts. Each teacher stands where he is and brings to his interpretation his own uniqueness. Each explanation is made from the frame of reference of the interpreter. Man can never fully comprehend the whole truth. At best his explanation is partial, fragmented, and imperfect.

A biblical selection such as Ephesians 4:31-32 can be used to verify this. A number of people are asked to write down their understanding of the meaning of the verse: What does the passage say? What does it mean? If the statement is applied to the individual life, what changes must be made? I tried this approach with friends for several evenings; everyone read his own understanding of the passage. There was a common thread running through all the interpretations, but there was an astonishing amount of diversity as each person saw the passage through his own eyes.

Dogmas, doctrines, and creeds express vividly and precisely generalizations of final truth perceived in particular instances of life. These perceptions are formulated verbally and expressed through a coherent system of thought and applied to life interpretations. They bring meaning to the values held by man. But dogmas are derived from partial perception of the total truth and distort truth by overemphasis of the partial as the absolute truth. Even the most astute perception cannot bear the final stamp of truth. "For our knowledge is imperfect and our prophecy is imperfect. . . . For now we see in a mirror dimly, but then face to face. Now I know in part; then I shall understand fully, even as I have been fully understood" (1 Cor. 13:9, 12).

When allegiance is to the letter and not the spirit; when loyalty is to the knowledge about God and not to God; when the freedom to doubt, to question, and to affirm is banned—then religion ceases to be a personal faith. Then man is merely parroting what someone else, however ably, has thought for him. This is why there are so many sects, factions, and dissensions in churches. Christians need to make room for differences in thinking and respect these diversities. The test or success of any truth is how well it can apply to the interpretation of life and make sense in terms of meaning, faith, direction, goal.

THE CHURCH AS AUTHORITY

A priest said to me, "If a layman asks me questions regarding matters of faith, I give him the answer of the church. I may disagree with the answer all the way but I am committed to endorse the church doctrine." The theory behind this is that the collective thinking and perceptive understanding of truth of a group of church fathers is bound to be better than individual thinking. This may well be if in each generation the doctrines of the church are tested in terms of real life situations. But doctrines are always shrouded and hidden in a great amount of mystery, which has a hold on the emotions of the believer but can freeze the mind.

Intelligent people who are ministered to by authoritarian

churches may try to resolve conflicts by compartmentalizing the matters of faith and life experiences and treating them as separate entities. Their faith and reason may be at odds with each other, but this does not seem to create any predicament. They feel neither obscurity nor enlightenment; in matters of faith they follow the leader.

But man may leave all windows open and let God's light shine through; he may listen to the word of God as the living word and listen to the interpretation of the word with great appreciation and respect; yet nothing may really happen until he quietly turns the searchlight inward. He lays bare his soul and tries to get rid of all the debris that blacks out the inner glory. His prayer is:

> Search me, O God, and know my heart!
> Try me and know my thoughts!
> And see if there be any wicked way in me,
> and lead me in the way everlasting!

> —Psalm 139:23-24

There is healing in the fellowship of such seekers and believers. There is strength and courage to go on because of the love one member feels for the other. Each grows in the awareness of the other because he recognizes in the other the "Eternal Thou" and his own is-ness.

THE AUTHORITY OF JESUS

We teachers have felt the power, the wisdom, and the love of God through the experiences of certain supreme men in history. They talk about their meetings with God and give us glimpses into the nature of God and the grounds of our being.

God's supreme and full revelation came to man through the life of Jesus Christ. God breathed into Jesus all that life is. When Jesus' disciples wrote his biography, they had all the facts they needed, and they added their own commentary. They projected themselves into the life of Jesus and often felt as he did; they identified themselves with him intimately and were aware of his concern for the realization of the kingdom of God within each person.

But the crucial question "Who do you say that I am?" must be answered by each person. It is not enough for him to quote other authorities; some say he is a great man, others say he is a wise teacher, still others say, he is "God of God, Light of Light, very God of very God, begotten, not made."[1] His soul will be restless until his answer comes from his own encounter with this man Jesus.

The four Gospels are a primary source of information; they are interesting and moving reading. *The Interpreter's Bible* clarifies obscure passages. The Gospels must be read several times and studied for a clear understanding of the thoughts of the Master. Jesus speaks in the silences of the Sea of Galilee, in the tumult of the marketplace, in the pressures of daily life, in the agony at the Garden of Gethsemane, in the anguish of the cross, and in the victory of the resurrection. The teacher hears—his answer will be alive and ring true just as Peter's did, "You are the Christ, the Son of the living God" (Matt. 16:16).

THE AUTHORITY OF MAN

The finite mind can never hope to make reliable statements about the nature of the Infinite Mind—it is beyond the scope of human understanding, so at best they are philosophical speculations. But man's heart has a certain intrinsic comprehension of the Supreme Being which enables him to respond to the Spirit of God. There is wisdom within the nature of things. Actual facts of life, when observed intelligently, can lead to generalizations

---

[1] From the Nicene Creed.

about the nature of the Infinite. Yet, no matter how profound the observation and analysis, the discovery is always partial. God said to Moses, "I am who I am." Martin Buber states, "In truth God may only be addressed and not expressed."[2]

A mother reported to me a conversation she overheard late one night between her seven-year-old Susan and her four-year-old Tom. They were wrestling with the question "Who made God?"

> *Tom:* Did God make trees?
> *Susan:* Yes, God made the trees.
> *Tom:* Did God make the sky?
> *Susan:* Yes, God made the sky.
> *Tom:* Is God bigger than Hercules?
> *Susan:* Yes, God is bigger than all supermen.
> *Tom:* Well, if God made everything, and he is bigger than everything, then God must have made himself.

"A bishop said to a small boy, 'Son, I'll give you a nickel if you can tell me where God is.' The youngster replied, 'Sir, I'll give you two nickels if you can tell me where he isn't.' "[3]

Bill listened to the tape that had recorded his sermon on Youth Sunday. We all sat in a semicircle facing him. He was to answer questions from the floor regarding ideas expressed in his talk. One of the leaders, most impressed with the quality and the sincerity of the sermon, asked, "Would you tell us how you arrived at these convictions? We worked together for the last four years; we wrestled with all kinds of problems. We were aware of your hunger for God, but now you sound as though you are at peace within yourself. Would you like to share your feelings with us?" Bill smiled and then looked very thoughtful. He said, "I was

---

[2] Martin Buber, *I and Thou* (New York: Charles Scribner's Sons, 1937), p. vii.

[3] Norman Ross, "This I Believe," *Chicago Daily News,* November 26, 1962, p. 3.

taking a walk with a friend when I asked him in desperation, 'How can I find God? Why after this long search have I not yet found God?' My friend replied, 'What you seek you have found already.' Suddenly I realized the significance and the magnitude of the truth, and I know that at that moment God and I found each other."

In that hushed moment everyone in the group realized the miracle of the visit of God and became aware of Bill's awareness of the "givenness of God." By some act of grace God wants man to want him. God understands the creatureliness of his creatures, the desperateness of the desperate, and the lostness of the lost. He wants to hallow man's hollowness. God can visit man through other individuals, regardless of their age.

IT MATTERS WHAT A TEACHER BELIEVES

Some people rely totally on the understanding of the mind. Faith, values, meanings have to be reduced to manageable units so they can be tested in laboratories or demonstrated by a mathematical formula. Another group relies solely on the understanding of the heart. They declare that faith needs no proof. It is QED. Still another group is alarmed by the dogmatic and defensive arguments on both sides and offers a third position. Faith, they declare, does not need to be against reason or heart. It belongs in the realm of the suprarational, the noumenal world. Faith is intuitive insight, concentrated wisdom, which has its origin in reason but goes beyond reason. It is a leap of the mind. There is the kind of knowing that makes two plus two equal four, and no one doubts it. There is another kind of knowing that humbles the teacher when a young child lifts up his face and says, "Teacher, I see the face of God in your face." No one doubts that either. Faith has its reasons which the mind can never fully comprehend.

Each teacher brings his varying beliefs to his teaching. Some teachers are unmoved movers. They are so confirmed in their theology that nothing new will touch them to widen their horizons. They affirm what was affirmed by their forefathers. They teach with a sense of urgency and a great zeal to gain converts to their way of thinking. If they need answers they merely call on the authority, "Tell me."

Other teachers rebel against the precise dogmatic indoctrination they received in their childhood, which left no room for doubting and reasoning. They maintain that religion must be more than a restating of traditional orthodoxy. They think of their search as a spiritual pilgrimage occasionally discovering a meaning; they guide the child to the open path of exploration. Each disclosure will lead gradually to their spiritual maturation, always perfecting but never attaining perfection. When a teacher has to do personal thinking and believing, it takes time. All important discoveries take time. And it is worth waiting for them. No one has yet found a shortcut to truth.

The Bible says: "As a man thinketh in his heart, so is he" (Prov. 23:7, KJV). And in *Maitri Upanishad* it is written: "For as one's thinking is, such one becomes, and it is because of this that thinking should be purified and transformed."[4]

It is important to empty the mind from time to time and take a fresh look at concepts strongly held through the years. Man must be exposed to new ideas through study, research, sharing, listening, and observation of life. No one can do this for a teacher, he must do it himself. God has given him intellect; it is his responsibility to use it.

Children come to the teacher with their questions and look up to him for authoritative answers. No one is fully prepared to undertake this tremendous responsibility, but it is better to be judged and condemned for imperfect wisdom than to be judged for blindness and neglect. Teachers who have a growing edge

---

[4] Quoted in Erich Fromm, *The Art of Loving* (New York: Harper & Bros., 1956), p. xiii.

will answer questions honestly and courageously. They say, "This is what I believe; what do you think?" "I do not know all the answers but I think——— or it may be that———." "I doubt if that is true. We may find the answer somewhere else. Let us look." "That is a new insight; how did you arrive at it?"

Every teacher must have a religious home in which he is not a stranger. He can then invite others to his home. Howard Thurman said at a retreat, "You must have a religious home somewhere to enable you to have a spiritual home everywhere. If you do not have a home somewhere, you do not have a home anywhere." Teachers must have convictions about their own faith but must leave an open end for further growth. Such teachers allow openness, honesty, acceptance in the discussions that go on in classrooms. In the final analysis freedom for independence of thought encourages interdependence and mutuality of thought. Each idea is listened to as though it were a unique contribution. The search for more light and truth must go on with faith and trust that God will reveal himself to those who seek him.

Mrs. Milton and her fifteen third-grade children worked together for three months to write a statement of faith. She listened to the questions of her children and felt strongly that just as she needed a religious home, children were looking for one too. The statement appeared on nine pages. They took each concept separately and spelled it out for themselves. Below are parts of the statement.

> I believe in God, the Father, who has made the world and all that is in it.
> I believe that God loves and cares for me and for all people.
> I believe that God is greater than anything else I know and yet always near.
> I believe that God can be depended upon and so I trust him.
> I believe that I should love God with all my heart and mind and soul and strength, and serve him all my days.

Jesus

I believe in Jesus Christ the Son of God, who came to show us what God is like and what we should be.

The Bible

I believe in the Bible as a record of God's dealing with men, showing us, as no other book does, how to live.

The Church

I believe in the church as a worldwide group of people joined together to worship God and to serve others in Christian ways.

Myself

I believe that I should live in the spirit of Jesus in thought and word and deed, to the end that the kingdom of God may come upon the earth.

I believe in God:
I know that the sky is blue—
    I can *see* it with my eyes.
I know that perfume smells good—
    I *smell* it with my nose.
I know that candy is sweet—
    I *taste* it with my tongue.
I know how the piano sounds—
    I *hear* it with my ears.
I know how velvet feels—
    I *feel* it with my touch.
These things I KNOW.

I believe in God:
I have not *seen* him.
I have not *smelled* him.
I have not *tasted* him.
I have not *heard* him.
I have not *felt* him with my hands.

I feel God deep inside of me:
I feel that he wants me to be *good.*
I feel that he wants me to be *happy.*
I feel that he wants me to *grow.*
I feel that he wants me to know the *joys of love.*
I feel that he wants me to be *wise and brave.*
   I see and smell and taste and hear
      and feel with my hands all that
      God has created in this world.
   This is how I learn to know more
      about God than just how I feel
      down inside.

This is how I believe in God.

When the teacher finds himself a member of the fellowship of seekers, he will begin to look for answers in various sources. He will find it useful to start a file under the main title of Theology with subtitles such as God, Jesus, Holy Spirit, Man, Sin, Salvation, Prayer, Eternal Life, Death. He will determine first his *own needs* and then think of the questions children ask for which he needs answers. He will start collecting material. He needs to read the Bible with specific questions in mind, always carrying a small notebook with him. If he finds an idea that appeals to him he will write it down, noting the source. He will add to his file clippings from articles, passages from books, poems that speak to him. He will look at his collection from time to time asking himself, "Do I agree with this idea? Why? Why not?" He will share his resources and his thinking with his friends over a cup of coffee in his home or in a discussion group. He will be amazed at his growing depth dimensions. Soon he will be too grown up to resort to the old-time favorite "Tell me." Each man must have a glimpse of visions of truth; each man has to take his own spiritual journey from knowledge to reflection, from reflection to faith, from faith to love, from love to the service of God and man.

The teacher will also want to study the creed or the statement of faith of his own church. Most churches will tell him that the creed is not a test of his faith but a testimony to his faith.

The teacher will want to read books that will help him to grow spiritually. His minister will be happy to lend books from his personal library, if they are not available in the church library.[5]

WAIT FOR THE LORD

They who wait for the Lord shall renew their strength,
    they shall mount up with wings like eagles,
they shall run and not be weary,
    they shall walk and not faint.

                        —Isaiah 40:31

We teachers may be impatient in our search, having an urge for arrival and an intense desire to find quickly a realization of our spirit in the Spirit of God, wherein we hope to discover our own image, the "uncreated" part of us, the essence of our being.

We are asked to wait for the Lord. This is a difficult discipline that demands an inner tranquillity, a quietness in the soul where all passions are at rest and geared to listening. While waiting we find that much of what we seek is already waiting for us. This is God's grace, our unmerited gift.

God calls us to himself and claims us as his own, loving, redeeming, forgiving, and transforming our lives through Jesus Christ, who is the true and full expression of the nature of God, the eternal Presence in every life and in every creative expression of life. He comes into our lives

> as one unknown, without a name, as of old, by the lakeside, he came to those men who knew him not. He speaks to us the same word: "Follow thou me!" and sets us to the tasks which

---

[5] See the Selected Bibliography, pp. 142 f.

he has to fulfill for our time. He commands. And to those who obey him, whether they be wise or simple, he will reveal himself in the toils, the conflicts, the sufferings which they shall pass through in his fellowship, and, as an ineffable mystery, they shall learn in their own experience who he is.[6]

---

[6] Albert Schweitzer, *The Quest of the Historical Jesus* (New York: Macmillan, 1948), p. 401.

Selected Bibliography

CHAPTER 1

Ashton-Warner, Sylvia. *Teacher.* New York: Simon & Schuster, 1963.

Chaplin, Dora P. *The Privilege of Teaching.* New York: Morehouse-Barlow, 1962.

Gibson, William. *The Miracle Worker.* New York: Bantam Books, 1962.

Goodykoontz, Harry G. and Betty L. *Training to Teach.* Philadelphia: Westminster Press, 1961.

Highet, Gilbert. *The Art of Teaching.* New York: Vintage Books, 1955.

Howe, Reuel L. *Man's Need and God's Action.* New York: Seabury Press, 1953.

——————. *The Miracle of Dialogue.* New York: Seabury Press, 1963.

Little, Sara. *Learning Together in the Christian Fellowship.* Richmond, Va.: John Knox Press, 1956.

Shinn, Roger Lincoln. *The Educational Mission of Our Church.* Philadelphia: United Church Press, 1962.

Wyckoff, D. Campbell. *The Task of Christian Education.* Philadelphia: Westminster Press, 1955.

CHAPTER 2

Carmichael, Leonard. *Manual of Child Psychology.* New York: Wiley & Sons, 1954.

Gesell, Arnold, and Ilg, Frances L. *Infant and Child in the Culture of Today*. New York: Harper & Bros., 1943.

Gruenberg, Sidonie M. (ed.). *Our Children Today*. New York: Viking, 1952.

Hartley, Ruth E., et al. *Understanding Children's Play*. New York: Columbia University Press, 1952.

Horney, Karen. *Our Inner Conflicts*. New York: W. W. Norton & Co., 1945.

Hymes, James L., Jr. *A Child Development Point of View*. New York: Prentice-Hall, 1955.

Jenkins, Gladys G., et al. *These Are Your Children*. Chicago: Scott, Foresman & Co., 1953.

Jersild, Arthur T. *Child Psychology* (5th ed.). New York: Prentice-Hall, 1960.

Sherrill, Lewis J. *The Struggle of the Soul*. New York: Macmillan, 1952.

——————. *Understanding Children*. Nashville: Abingdon Press, 1939.

Strang, Ruth. *The Role of the Teacher in Personnel Work* (4th rev. ed.). New York: Teachers College, Columbia University, 1953.

CHAPTER 3

Anderson, Phoebe M. *Religious Living with Nursery Children*. Philadelphia: United Church Press, 1956.

Bowman, Clarice. *Ways Youth Learn*. New York: Harper & Bros., 1952.

Bruner, Jerome S. *On Knowing: Essays for the Left Hand*. Cambridge, Mass.: Harvard University Press, 1962.

Cornell, Alice E. *Teaching Junior Highs*. Valley Forge, Pa.: Judson Press, 1959.

Ferguson, Rowena. *The Church's Ministry with Senior Highs*. Nashville: Abingdon Press, 1963.

Heron, Frances D. *Kathy Ann, Kindergartner*. Nashville: Abingdon Press, 1955.

Hill, Dorothy La Croix. *Working with Juniors at Church*. Nashville: Abingdon Press, 1955.

Lee, Florence B. *Teaching Primary Children*. Valley Forge, Pa.: Judson Press, 1951.

CHAPTER 4

Hocking, William Ernest. *The Coming World Civilization.* New York: Harper & Bros., 1956.

The Interpreter's Bible (12 vols.). Nashville: Abingdon Press, 1963.

Lobingier, John L. *The Better Church School.* Philadelphia: United Church Press, 1952.

——————. *If Teaching Is Your Job.* Philadelphia: United Church Press, 1956.

McKibben, Frank M. *Guiding Workers in Christian Education.* Nashville: Abingdon Press, 1953.

Taylor, Marvin J. (ed.). *Religious Education.* Nashville: Abingdon Press, 1960.

Vieth, Paul H. *The Church School.* Philadelphia: United Church Press, 1957.

CHAPTER 5

Allstrom, Elizabeth. *Let's Play a Story.* New York: Friendship Press, 1957.

Baxter, Edna M. *Teaching the New Testament.* Philadelphia: United Church Press, 1960.

Bowman, Atha S. *You Can Do It.* Valley Forge, Pa.: Judson Press, 1950.

Brown, Jeanette P. *The Storyteller in Religious Education.* Philadelphia: United Church Press, 1951.

Carr, Constance (ed.). *Art for Children's Growing.* Washington, D. C.: Association for Childhood Education International (3615 Wisconsin Avenue N.W.), 1955.

Cole, Natalie Robinson. *The Arts in the Classroom.* New York: John Day Co., 1940.

D'Amico, Victor, et al. *Art for the Family.* Garden City, N. Y.: Doubleday, 1958.

Eversole, Finley (ed.). *Christian Faith and the Contemporary Arts.* Nashville: Abingdon Press, 1962.

Keiser, Armilda B. *Here's How and When* (rev. ed.). New York: Friendship Press, 1960.

Lobingier, Elizabeth M. *Activities in Child Education*. Philadelphia: United Church Press, 1950.

Lowenfeld, Viktor, and Brittain, W. Lambert. *Creative and Mental Growth* (4th ed.). New York: Macmillan, 1964.

McClinton, Katharine Morrison. *Christian Art Through the Ages*. New York: Macmillan, 1962.

Morrison, Eleanor, and Foster, Virgil. *Creative Teaching in the Church*. Englewood Cliffs, N. J.: Prentice-Hall, 1963.

Nichols, Hildred, and Williams, Lois. *Learning About Role-Playing for Children and Teachers*. Washington, D. C.: Association for Childhood Education International (3615 Wisconsin Avenue N.W.), 1960.

Rice, Rebecca. *Creative Activities*. Philadelphia: United Church Press, 1947.

Rumpf, Oscar J. *The Use of Audio Visuals in the Church*. Philadelphia: United Church Press, 1958.

Tower, Howard E. *Church Use of Audio Visuals* (rev. ed.). Nashville: Abingdon Press, 1959.

CHAPTER 6

Abba, Raymond. *Principles of Christian Worship*. New York: Oxford University Press, 1957.

Bailey, J. Martin and Betty Jane. *Worship with Youth*. Philadelphia: United Church Press, 1962.

Baxter, Edna M. *Learning to Worship*. Valley Forge, Pa.: Judson Press, 1965.

Bowman, Clarice M. *Resources for Worship*. New York: Association Press, 1961.

Brenner, Scott Francis. *The Art of Worship*. New York: Macmillan, 1961.

Brown, Edgar S., Jr. *Living the Liturgy*. Philadelphia: Fortress Press, 1961.

Brown, Jeanette P. *Children's Worship in the Church School*. New York: Harper & Bros., 1939.

Curry, Louise H., and Wetzel, Chester M. *Worship Services Using the Arts*. Philadelphia: Westminster Press, 1961.

Fauth, Robert T. *When We Worship*. Philadelphia: United Church Press, 1961.

Fisk, Margaret Palmer. *Look Up and Live*. St. Paul: Macalaster Park Publishing Co., 1953.

Hedley, George P. *When Protestants Worship*. Nashville: Abingdon Press, 1961.

Horton, Douglas. *The Meaning of Worship*. New York: Harper & Bros., 1959.

Hymns for Junior Worship. Philadelphia: Westminster Press, 1940.

Hymns for Primary Worship. Philadelphia: Westminster Press, 1946.

Phillips, Dorothy B., et al. (eds.). *The Choice Is Always Ours*. New York: Harper & Bros., 1960.

Rest, Friedrich. *Our Christian Symbols*. Philadelphia: United Church Press, 1954.

Ritter, Richard H. *The Arts of the Church*. Philadelphia: United Church Press, 1947.

Taylor, Margaret Fisk. *Symbolic Dance and Worship*. Philadelphia: United Church Press, 1967.

——————. *Time for Discovery*. Philadelphia: United Church Press, 1964.

——————. *Time for Wonder*. Philadelphia: United Church Press, 1959.

Thomas, Edith Lovell. *Music in Christian Education*. Nashville: Abingdon Press, 1953.

Vieth, Paul H. *Worship in Christian Education*. Philadelphia: United Church Press, 1965.

Williams, John G. *Worship and the Modern Child*. New York: Seabury Press, 1957.

CHAPTER 7

Brown, Robert McAfee. *The Significance of the Church*. Philadelphia: Westminster Press, 1956.

Eisenberg, Helen and Larry. *Omnibus of Fun*. New York: Association Press, 1956.

Fox, Henry W. *The Child's Approach to Religion*. New York: Harper & Bros., 1945.

Harbin, Elvin O. *The Fun Encyclopedia.* Nashville: Abingdon Press, 1940.

Hunter, Edith F. *The Family Finds Out.* Boston: Beacon Press, 1951.

Miller, Randolph Crump. *Your Child's Religion.* Garden City, N. Y.: Doubleday, 1962.

Phillips, J. B. *Is God at Home?* Nashville: Abingdon Press, 1957.

Powell, Oliver. *Household of Power.* Philadelphia: United Church Press, 1962.

Trueblood, Elton and Pauline. *The Recovery of Family Life.* New York: Harper & Bros., 1953.

Widmer, Frederick W. *How Home and Church Can Work Together.* Richmond, Va.: John Knox Press, 1960.

Wynn, John C. *How Christian Parents Face Family Problems.* Philadelphia: Westminster Press, 1955.

CHAPTER 8

Allport, Gordon W. *Becoming.* New Haven: Yale University Press, 1955.

Baruch, Dorothy W. *New Ways in Discipline.* New York: McGraw-Hill, 1949.

Feelings and Learning. Washington, D. C.: Association for Childhood Education International (3615 Wisconsin Avenue N.W.), 1965.

Fromm, Erich. *The Art of Loving.* New York: Harper & Bros., 1956.

Harner, Nevin C. *About Myself.* Philadelphia: United Church Press, 1950.

Hymes, James L., Jr. *Discipline.* New York: Teachers College, Columbia University, 1949.

Jersild, Arthur T. *When Teachers Face Themselves.* New York: Teachers College, Columbia University, 1955.

Künkel, Fritz. *My Dear Ego.* Philadelphia: United Church Press, 1947.

Redl, Fritz. *Understanding Children's Behavior.* New York: Teachers College, Columbia University, 1957.

Tournier, Paul. *The Meaning of Persons.* New York: Harper & Bros., 1957.

Wittenberg, Rudolph M. *The Art of Group Discipline.* New York: Association Press, 1951.

CHAPTER 9

Baillie, Donald M. *God Was in Christ*. New York: Charles Scribner's Sons, 1948.

Baillie, John. *A Diary of Readings*. New York: Charles Scribner's Sons, 1955.

Bonhoeffer, Dietrich. *Life Together*. New York: Harper & Bros., 1954.

Bro, Margueritte Harmon. *When Children Ask* (rev. ed.). New York: Harper & Bros., 1956.

Buber, Martin. *I and Thou* (2d ed.). New York: Charles Scribner's Sons, 1958.

Casteel, John L. (ed.). *Spiritual Renewal Through Personal Groups*. New York: Association Press, 1957.

Ferré, Nels F. S. *Know Your Faith*. New York: Harper & Bros., 1959.

—————. *Strengthening the Spiritual Life*. New York: Harper & Bros., 1951.

Finegan, Jack. *Youth Asks About Religion*. New York: Association Press, 1949.

Fosdick, Harry Emerson. *Dear Mr. Brown*. New York: Harper & Bros., 1961.

—————. *Riverside Sermons*. New York: Harper & Bros., 1958.

Frankl, Viktor. *From Death-Camp to Existentialism*. Boston: Beacon Press, 1959.

Goodenough, E. W. *Toward a Mature Faith*. New Haven: Yale University Press, 1961.

Gordon, Ernest. *Through the Valley of the Kwai*. New York: Harper & Bros., 1962.

Harner, Nevin C. *I Believe*. Philadelphia: United Church Press, 1950.

Isherwood, Margaret. *Faith Without Dogma*. New York: Harper & Row, 1964.

Jones, Mary Alice. *Tell Me About God*. Chicago: Rand McNally, 1943.

—————. *Tell Me About Heaven*. Chicago: Rand McNally, 1956.

—————. *Tell Me About Jesus*. Chicago: Rand McNally, 1944.

—————. *Tell Me About Prayer*. Chicago: Rand McNally, 1948.

—————. *Tell Me About the Bible*. Chicago: Rand McNally, 1945.

Kelly, Thomas. *A Testament of Devotion*. New York: Harper & Bros., 1941.

Khoobyar, Helen. *Facing Adult Problems in Christian Education*. Philadelphia: Westminster Press, 1963.

Miller, Randolph Crump. *Biblical Theology and Christian Education*. New York: Charles Scribner's Sons, 1956.

Schweitzer, Albert. *Out of My Life and Thought*. New York: Holt, Rinehart & Winston, 1949.

Shinn, Roger Lincoln, and Williams, Daniel Day. *We Believe: An Interpretation of the United Church Statement of Faith*. Philadelphia: United Church Press, 1966.

Thurman, Howard. *Deep Is the Hunger*. New York: Harper & Bros., 1951.

——————. *Disciplines of the Spirit*. New York: Harper & Row, 1963.

——————. *The Growing Edge*. New York: Harper & Bros., 1956.

——————. *The Inward Journey*. New York: Harper & Bros., 1961.

——————. *Meditations of the Heart*. New York: Harper & Bros, 1953.

Tillich, Paul. *Dynamics of Faith*. New York: Harper & Bros., 1957.

Trueblood, Elton. *The Company of the Committed*. New York: Harper & Bros., 1961.

Underhill, Evelyn. *The Spiritual Life*. New York: Harper & Bros., 1955.

Walpole, Ellen W. *Why Should I?* New York: Harper & Bros., 1949.

Walsh, Chad. *Campus Gods on Trial* (rev. ed.). New York: Macmillan, 1962.

Wickenden, Arthur C. *The Concerns of Religion*. New York: Harper & Bros., 1959.